World Paperweights:
Millefiori & Lampwork

Robert G. Hall

Schiffer Publishing Ltd ®

4880 Lower Valley Road, Atglen, PA 19310 USA

Dedication

This book is dedicated to my two sons, Richard and Peter, who are showing encouraging signs of becoming paperweight collectors.

Designed by John P. Cheek
Cover design by Bruce M. Waters
Type set in Zapf Chancery Bd BT/Souvenir Lt BT

ISBN: 0-7643-1349-5
Printed in China
1 2 3 4

Published by Schiffer Publishing Ltd.
4880 Lower Valley Road
Atglen, PA 19310
Phone: (610) 593-1777; Fax: (610) 593-2002
E-mail: Schifferbk@aol.com
Please visit our web site catalog at
www.schifferbooks.com
We are always looking for people to write books on new and related subjects. If you have an idea for a book please contact us at the above address.

This book may be purchased from the publisher.
Include $3.95 for shipping.
Please try your bookstore first.
You may write for a free catalog.

In Europe, Schiffer books are distributed by
Bushwood Books
6 Marksbury Ave.
Kew Gardens
Surrey TW9 4JF England
Phone: 44 (0) 20 8392-8585;
Fax: 44 (0) 20 8392-9876
E-mail: Bushwd@aol.com
Free postage in the U.K., Europe; air mail at cost.

Contents

Acknowledgments
A Special Thanks

A big thank you goes to two American dealers and their wives who by their help and generosity have made this book so much easier to compile.

Gary and Marge McClanahan have been collecting paperweights for as long as they can remember and have amassed a collection that numbers well over two thousand. These weights vary in value from a few dollars to almost priceless pieces that they could not part with. Their collection encompasses every type, shape, and size of paperweight from every era and country that has ever produced them.

After serving as a military pilot, Gary joined American Airlines as a commercial pilot and in this capacity he was able to schedule his flying duties to coincide with the major paperweight and antiques shows around the United States, where he and Marge could buy, sell, and exchange to their hearts content. Gary is considered to be one of the worlds foremost paperweight dealers and a most knowledgeable public speaker, on all things related to paperweights, and in particular on paperweights produced in the American Midwest. His grasp of the complex histories surrounding these glassworks and the people involved in the production leaving these factories by the front and back doors — made by fathers and sons, mothers and daughters, uncles, aunts, and just about everybody else who worked in the glass business — is admirable. I listened to Gary delivering his talk on paperweights made in the Midwest at the PCA convention in 1997 and knew he could help me with information in difficult areas of paperweight collecting.

Paul and Karen Dunlop have become extremely well known throughout the paperweight world as dealers and collectors of the highest caliber. Their personal collection of antique and very rare paperweights is, perhaps, one of the finest in the world.

When asked if they could help with photographs of rarer examples from Pantin, Saint Mandé, Val-Saint-Lambert, and Bohemia, the answer was how many do you need? They have gathered together fine examples of all the French, English, American, and other European makers to compliment their very extensive private collection and stock for sale as paperweight dealers.

Paul is also a knowledgeable speaker on the paperweight circuit, and after listening to him speak on Clichy color grounds at the same PCA convention in 1997, I have personally begun a collection of these weights.

Paul and Karen travel the USA for three months every year, covering thousands of miles in their motor home, visiting shows, collectors, and dealers and, despite having a large amount of stock stolen, were soon back in business with fresh paperweights to meet the increasing demand from their clients.

My grateful thanks to all the people who have loaned photographs and allowed their paperweights to be shown in this book.

With an extra special thanks to Joan Pettifor who, despite illness, finished the proof reading on time and Andy Barboro, who keeps the computer running and virus free.

Anne Anderson
Rick Ayotte
Roy and Pam Brown
Caithness Glass Ltd.
Cambridge Paperweight Circle Members
Terry and Hilary Johnson
Zvi Klemer
Colin and Debbie Mahoney
William Manson and Family
AnneMarie and Gerd Mattes
Gillian Murray
Brian Musselwhite, Royal Ontario Museum
Perthshire Paperweights Ltd.
Alastair and Nora Petrie
Portia Gallery
Margaret Preston
Selkirk Glass Ltd.
Larry Selman
Sothebys of London
Colin Terris
The Vienna Art Auctions, Palais Kinsky
Bill Volkman

Introduction

This book is written for the benefit of accomplished paperweight collectors and newer people, whose hobby of collecting is enhanced by being able to see and compare their own weights with others of the same style and makers, regardless of how modest their collection. As a collector I like nothing better than to peruse a book full of photographs on paperweights, my favorite subject. I enjoy looking and admiring all types of weights and reading of the makers history, be they antique or modern. I have tried to show examples of the finest and the more modest paperweights from the last one hundred and fifty years, as it is not always the most expensive weight which has interest and can captivate a collector, even weights costing little more than a few dollars today, can become collectible and sought after.

I have been able to show the works of the lesser known French makers Saint Mandé and Pantin, plus chapters on the wonderfully detailed lampwork of the Russian made paperweights. There are major chapters on the antique Venetian and Bohemian paperweights, with photographs of the current production weights made on the island of Murano. Another chapter shows the copying ability of the 1930s Chinese makers with examples of French and American antiques and their modern copies. Further examples from today's Chinese factories demonstrate the improving quality of their glass and workmanship. Some of these weights, costing just a few dollars, are of a gift nature and not intended for the collecting market; but today, copies are being made of French nineteenth century antique paperweights, some arriving from China and some being made elsewhere. Many are of a quality that could, and has, deceived dealers and collectors alike. Although it is not the intention of the large glasshouses to deceive, they just produce paperweights in *the style of*, once these better made copies arrive on to the secondary market its at this point that unscrupulous people can take advantage of collectors, especially with the advent of the worldwide internet auction houses, where collectors do not get the chance to inspect the weights personally.

Glass was first made around 3000 years BC, but the paperweight art form does not appear until the mid-nineteenth century. It is still arguable as to who made the first true paperweight designed to hold down loose sheets of paper, but the prime contenders are almost certainly Italy and the Bohemian region of Europe.

Millefiori beads would appear to be the earliest connection to paperweights. Multicolored examples have been found in Egyptian and Chinese tombs from around the third century BC. Many pieces of Roman glass have been found with millefiori sections embedded within the designs of vases and bowls. A third century BC mosaic vessel that was found in an excavated tomb in Canosa, Italy, has sections of colored canes with a white spiral and yellow center on a blue ground and sections of encased gold foil embedded in the design. Italians have used millefiori canes for decoration from ancient times right up to the present day with production being centered around Venice and the island of Murano. The present day production of millefiori canes in Murano is probably the largest in the world, with millefiori canes being exported worldwide for inclusion in paperweights and related objects.

The techniques of shaping glass at a blow lamp have been known for several hundred years but it is only since the middle of the nineteenth century that it was perfected to the point that paperweights with lampwork inclusions became such sought after collectibles. The designs, incorporating flowers, butterflies, and various animals, were made at the French glasshouses of Pantin, Baccarat, Saint Mandé, Clichy, and St. Louis. Consistency was achieved to the point where even with today's technology, much of the workmanship has never been surpassed. Today, a select few American studio artists have attained a degree of perfection that does stand comparison with the nineteenth century paperweight makers and their works are highly collectible and sought by museums, galleries, and collectors alike.

About the Price Guide

The prices have been calculated at $1.5 dollars to a pound Sterling only as a rough guide due to the considerable fluctuation in European currencies in 1999 and 2000. In some cases I have anticipated the price some weights may achieve as they rarely show up at auction. The author accepts no responsibility for paperweights that may or may not sell for the values stated in this book.

Glossary
Commonly Used Terms
Relating to Paperweights

Annealing. All paperweights and glass articles must be cooled very slowly, the time depending on the mass of the article concerned. A paperweight would be left in a slowly cooling oven for approximately 24 hours. This slow cooling process prevents cracking of the glass.

Air Bubbles. Silvery air bubbles can be added to the inside of a paperweight, as seen in a dump weight, by piercing the still soft glass with a sharp steel pin or steel comb. This traps a small amount of air inside, and when the pin is withdrawn, closing the hole, the trapped air will expand on reheating the glass.

Baccarat, French Glasshouse. Perhaps the most famous of paperweight makers in the nineteenth century, and still producing quality paperweights and millefiori objects today.

Basal Ring. This refers to that part of the paperweight base, which touches the surface that the paperweight is resting on. When a paperweight has its pontil mark removed by grinding, a shallow depression is formed which usually extends outward toward the edge, leaving a flat area of approximately 0.25 inch to rest upon. This prevents scratching and obscuring the canework beneath the paperweight.

Basket. A basket describes the outer row of canes drawn down and beneath the paperweight, enclosing the bottom half of the weight.

Batch. After the sand and other ingredients are melted down in the furnace, the glass becomes known and referred to as "the batch."

Billet. A lump or slug of clear glass.

Bohemia. An area that includes Czechoslovakia and much of Eastern Europe which produced glassware and paperweights in the classic period.

Button. "On the button" is a term used to describe the set up of canes after they have been removed from the steel or iron mold. Not being much bigger than a button, the magnifying property of the glass dome on a paperweight enlarges the button to make it fill out the weight.

Canes. The basic element in the majority of concentric paperweights. Pliable glass of a single color is drawn out by two glassworkers attaching a pontil rod on either end of a lump of glass approximately three inches in diameter and six inches long. The workers will then move away from each other, holding the glass three feet above the floor. As the glass is pulled in two directions, the center reduces down to approximately 0.25 inch and cools. The cane continues to be drawn out to forty or fifty feet in length. After thirty seconds to allow cooling, the rod is laid on the floor and cut into one foot lengths with pincers.

Carpet Ground. This description applies when the same canes are used to cover the bottom element of the paperweight. Usually other, more colorful canes, will then be set into this "carpet."

Classic Period. Any paperweights described as from "the classic period" were made around 1845 to 1852. This was the height of the English and French paperweight popularity, when most of the quality pieces were made.

Clichy. French Glasshouse. A major producer of superior quality paperweights in the nineteenth century.

Close Packed. Canes bundled together and held in no particular order or pattern before being encased in the final covering of glass.

Cog Cane. This can be a simple one color rod, formed in a serrated mold, and may be the base for a more complex cane.

Complex Cane. This is a combination of many smaller rods and canes, as many as one hundred bundled together, reheated and drawn out to miniaturize the combined rods and canes to a cane of normal size. A magnifying glass is then required to appreciate its complexity.

Concentric. The majority of English paperweights were "concentrics." From a central large cane, rings of ever increasing circles of millefiori canes reach out to the edge of the weight. Usually five or six rows, but as many as eight rows can been found.

Crib. A crib is a word used to describe a small glassworks, usually at the glassmakers home and worked by one or two people.

Cushion. The canes are set in rings of metal before being picked up by the soft glass on the end of a pontil rod. This gives the appearance of a pin cushion.

Dipping. This was a method of covering and adding a further amount of colored glass to overlay a paperweight. The weight was dipped into the required color to pick up just sufficient to cover the top, this added glass was then pulled and pushed all over the object with the worker's pliers and tweezers-type tools, to create a thin layer of a different color. The object is then reheated and smoothed off. Further coats can then be added.

Facet. Many weights were cut on the sides and top to allow the viewer an unobstructed view of the internal motif. This could be a flat or concave cut of approximately 1 inch.

Flash. This is a thin layer of colored glass sometimes applied all over, or just to the base of a weight. If applied all over, windows are normally cut to allow viewing inside the weight, as with an overlay weight.

Foot. Paperweights and inkwells have this feature to break up the outline. The foot is created by applied pressure with a pair of steel tongs while the glass is still soft.

Frigger. Friggers are pieces of work made by the glassworkers, with and without the knowledge of the management. The purpose could be to use up waste glass, expand on skills and new techniques, or for use as gifts for family and friends.

Gather. A gather of glass is a lump of molten glass, taken from the furnace, to form another part of the paperweight, such as the dome.

Glory Hole. This refers to the entrance opening of the glass furnace where paperweights can be reheated to a working temperature.

Latticinio or Lace. Normal diameter rods with spiral twists of white or colored threads, with the length being longer than the diameter, sometimes used as a base on which other millefiori canes are set.

Lampwork. This is the method used to create flowers and other worked items, using a small torch with a gas and oxygen mixture and a small, fine hot flame. Glass can be worked into any shape imaginable.

Magnum. This refers to the size given to a paperweight that is of a larger diameter than normal, usually over 3.75 inches.

Marver Plate. This is a solid steel plate used by the glassworkers to roll out and shape the soft glass. It is on this plate that the glass can become contaminated with dust and dirt, and although not seen while the glass is in this semi molten stage, particles of dirt show up in a magnified version when the paperweight is cold.

Millefiori. Originating in Italy, millefiori means a thousand flowers, as most millefiori canes are said to look like flower heads. Millefiori canes were first used in glass from the 2nd century AD.

Overlay. The paperweight has further colored glass added to encase the outside of the weight which can then be cut with windows, to allow the insides to be seen.

Pontil Rod and Mark. This is a steel rod that can be hollow to allow air to be blown through, in order to expand the glass in size, and to gather the glass from the furnace. The paperweight is formed and worked while attached to this rod. When the weight is ready to be detached from the pontil rod, air is gently blown on the stem of glass attached to the paperweight, this cooling allows the glassworker to tap the rod sharply, allowing the finished paperweight to fall into a soft flame resistant material, after which it is taken immediately to the annealing oven. When cool and annealed, the rough mark where the weight was attached to the rod is removed by grinding. Many glasshouses never removed this mark if it did not protrude below the base of the weight.

Pastry Mold Cane. This cane is usually deeply serrated with the bottom being flared out larger than the top, as with a ladies skirt.

Ridge mark. When the cane set up is picked up from the steel or iron mold, by a gather of glass, the two halves stick together and usually leave an indentation where the two halves meet. This is quite common on English paperweights.

Set ups. This describes the millefiori canes that have been cut to the desired lengths, usually about 1/4 of an inch, which are then sorted into size and design, and with the help of tweezers placed into a steel or iron ring mold with a base. The designs are set in concentric circles, starting from the outside edge, and with ever decreasing circles towards the center where usually a much larger cane will be used to centralize the set up.

Silhouette Cane. Heads and animals are the usual subjects in these canes that are viewed in cross section after molding, and being drawn out and cut.

Spaced Millefiori. Where canes are placed in the paperweight in a non-geometric pattern but with spaces between them.

Saint Louis. A notable French Glasshouse which produced paperweights and related glassware in the classic period, especially fine concentrics.

Striae. This word is used to describe the stress lines that can sometimes be seen in glass paperweights. The almost transparent lines are caused by the near molten glass being twisted and turned in the working process. Occasionally these lines are on the surface, caused by pressure on the dome by the tools used to smooth and shape the final gather of glass. The lines may be felt with the tips of the fingers if on the surface, like slight ripples, and can cause distortion to the motif inside the weight. However, they can be polished out if on the surface, but nothing can be done with internal lines.

Sulphide. A molded ceramic glass paste portrait of a famous person which is then encased in a gather of glass to form a paperweight, or for decorating other objects.

Torsade. A twisted cane that normally encircles the bottom of a paperweight like a rope.

Making a Paperweight by the American Method

Traditionally glass is gathered from a furnace of molten glass by the glassworker on the end of his pontil rod. This method works fine for quantity producers of paperweights such as Perthshire Paperweights, but for the studio artists of America who may only produce two or three weights a week, it is not cost effective to have the pot of molten glass simmering away for weeks on end to cater for their small needs.

Adapting skills learned during his years working for the American scientific glass blowing industry, Rick Ayotte — one of America's foremost paperweight makers — has perfected the glass billet method to encase lampwork within a body of glass. The billet of crystal glass is of optical quality and provides the finished weight with superb magnifying properties that enhances the internal subject.

The process from start to finish entails hundreds of separate actions and to photograph every one would fill this book. I photographed Rick from his early start at 5:30 am to the eventual finish with the weight being placed in the annealing oven by an exhausted Rick in the late evening. Even though the weight is finished, it is with trepidation that Rick opens the oven next day to check that the piece meets his very high standards. Not all paperweights will be flawless and many are destined for the trash bin due to small imperfections within the glass.

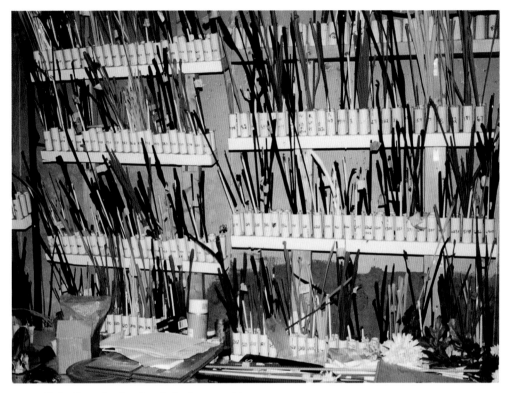

Selection of colored rods for lampworking.
A small selection of colored rods that line the walls of Rick Ayottes workshop. Rods are tried and tested from manufacturers all over the world in Rick's quest for color reality in his work. The coefficient of the glass rods have to be within a tight band, otherwise the different contraction properties of the glass cause annealing cracks within the design.

The Beginning.
Rick starts the long process in making a paperweight with the preparation of the component parts. The petals, leaves, and anything else that is to be encased is meticulously finished at the lamp. The word lamp, in antiquity, refers to a small container filled with a flammable oil which is exuded through a small nozzle and lit. When forced air is added at the nozzle, an intense heat can be created that is sufficient to melt glass. This method was used until the advent of natural gas and propane tanks. In this case, Rick uses a fine propane gas jet. Artistry, dexterity, and extreme patience is the key to Rick's success in this challenging art form.

Assembling the Components.
With a fine jet to weld the individual parts together, the petals are kept at an even temperature on a hot plate until needed. The layers of flower petals are gradually built up, and in this bloom a dragonfly is skillfully inserted between the petals. The petals are graduated to a small size near the top to create a slowly opening Dahlia.

The building up of the flower.
With as many as nine or ten petal layers, the smaller petals are built around the stamen in ever increasing size. The encasing process would distort these smaller petals if they were just added layer upon layer for nine or ten levels with the possibility of air bubbles being trapped between the petals.

Joining the small and larger petals.
With the smaller petals and stamen attached to a clear glass rod, the center portion of the Dahlia is gently secured to the larger base petals. Satisfied with the perfectly aligned petals, the lampworked part of the operation is now ready for the encasing process.

9

Heating the billet.
Continuously rotating the billet ensures the glass is
evenly heated to the point where it is soft and
elastic to enable the lampwork to be pressed into
the billet without distorting the design.

Attaching the petal set up to the billet.
The flower head was constructed in two parts. In this photo,
the set up with the smaller petals has already been attached
to the large petals, which in turn are then covered with the
almost liquid glass billet.

Reheating to shape the billet.
With the flower safely encased, Rick returns to
the bench to begin reheating the billet before
the final shaping of the paperweight.

Shaping the paperweight.
Using a *steel* mold, the weight is shaped to the desired size and contour. At this stage any excess glass and surface impurities can be removed.

A final check before the weight is removed from the pontil rod.
Rick checks the paperweight in fine detail before the weight is allowed to begin the cooling process in the annealing oven.

Fire polishing the finished paperweight.
This method ensures that all irregularities on the surface of the weight are removed and smoothed to a fine finish.

The finished paperweight.
The finished paperweight is a fine yellow dahlia with a dragonfly sitting on a petal. This superb example demonstrates not only the days work to achieve this result but many countless hours of trial and error before skill, artistry, and patience are finally rewarded with a masterpiece in glass, frozen in time forever.

Italian Paperweights

It was thought that the Venetian glassmakers of Italy, or possibly their near neighbors across the Adriatic Sea in Bohemia, were the first to make paperweights that were made for the express use of holding down paper. The Venetian, Pietro Bigaglia (1786-1876) is the most likely candidate as the first man to make a paperweight with millefiori inclusions. Dated 1845 paperweights are known with a PB signature cane which would suggest he was making paperweights before 1845 as part of his learning experience. The ancient Romans were certainly using millefiori and mosaic pieces of glass to decorate bowls and vases, from as early as the third century BC and although crude in construction, by today's high standards, the techniques used by the early Romans would have been very similar to today's production of glass with encased millefiori canes. Soda crystal had been invented around 1450 by Angelo Barovier, whose family business still makes glass today on Murano.

The story of the Venetian paperweight begins with the exile in 1291 of all the glassworkers in Venice to the tiny island of Murano, about a mile offshore in the lagoon of Venice. The serious risk of fire to the Venetian city was enough for the city fathers to force all the glassworkers to relocate and rebuild their glasshouses on Murano. This move also helped to confine the movement of workers and their specialized and secret knowledge of working the glass to a small area. The prized skills of glassmaking were rigorously protected by the threat of death for any transgressors, but even with this threat the Venetian's jealously guarded secrets did eventually spread throughout the rest of Europe.

The Venetians were very successful in the production of decorative ware and especially in the use of Latticinio and threaded or spiral glass canes. Latticinio comes from the Italian word for milk, latte, meaning milky or white glass. Millefiori is also from the Italian language, meaning thousand flowers and is often referred to as murrine. This term is used to describe a glass cane which is constructed using other glass rods to make a pattern that runs through the cane when reheated and stretched. This can then be sliced into segments. The first paperweights were probably derived from glass balls which had been made in Venice from as early as the fifteenth century. These balls had millefiori segments encased within and were recorded by Marcus Sabellicus around 1495 in *De Situ Urbis Venetiae*, whose expression *flowers that clothe the spring meadows* means so much to all paperweight collectors as a description that personifies the glass paperweight. These glass balls are thought to have been used as hand coolers by the refined ladies of the court society from Roman times. It is only a short step of progression from the hand cooler to the paperweight that we know today; indeed, modern glasshouses are once again making hand coolers for decorative use.

The Venetian craftsmen of the nineteenth century were renowned and unsurpassed for their use of millefiori in all sorts of objects, with the Franchini and Bigaglia families being the main exponents of this art form. Giovanni Battista Franchini (1804-1873) is known to have made handles, scent bottles, and plaques using millefiori and lampwork, and with an occasional dated piece. His son Giacomo (1827-1897) also made portrait canes. G. B. Franchini began making very beautiful and complex millefiori canes, possibly as early as 1840, and had sold canes to Pietro Bigaglia. His success with millefiori encouraged Franchini to develop this skill further and his experimentation eventually led to the remarkable canes containing portraits, the Rialto bridge, gondolas, birds, and animals. These canes were used in many different objects that include handles, beads, seals, doorknobs, and paperweights.

Pietro Bigaglia (1786-1876) also made paperweights that were good enough to win a gold medal at the 1845 Vienna exhibition. The most common and commercial type of weight he made was constructed using many short lengths of latticinio and twisted cane, all encased within a gather of glass which could be described as an end of day weight. Little thought went into the construction of these pieces as they were often made with a very shallow dome of glass that is insufficient to magnify and enhance the colorful canes within. The surface is left with an uneven and bobble texture and the weight usually has a less than perfect diameter. I have seen some of these crude weights that are almost oval in appearance. Very occasionally, even these commercial and mass produced weights can enclose an odd better cane such as a checker board or rose cane. The better canes were used in his high quality weights which included many faces of well known dignitaries and characters from the arts, as well as the aforementioned animals, gondolas, and even the Rialto bridge. These weights are some of the most highly sought after by collectors which may be dated and signed but are extremely rare.

Illustration from De Re Metallica.
The workware and bare feet may have changed but the furnaces and techniques have changed very little since this illustration was produced in the fifteenth century. Many of the items seen in the illustration such as blowing irons, marver plates, iron tongs, and molds are very similar to the pieces used by today's glassmaker.

The Island of Murano.
The island of Murano is about a square mile in size and lies approximately a mile out in the Lagoon of Venice. Almost all of the land mass is built upon, with houses and glass factories, and with several canals dissecting the island.

A Murano canal.
The glasshouses are easily accessible by foot and boat, the ferry in this photograph calls right to the door of several glassworks. The foothills of the Dolomites can be seen snow-capped in the background of this photograph. My visit to Murano took place in February when very few visitors were about on the island, unlike in the main city of Venice which is crowded with tourists twelve months of the year.

Canal-side scene in Murano.
This scene has changed little in hundreds of years. Remove the TV aerials and it is easy to step back to the early days of paperweight making.

The Barovier & Toso Showrooms.
On the side of this canal is the front showrooms of the Barovier & Toso glassworks. The showrooms of all the glasshouses can be overwhelming in size and the variety of glass they produce. The bigger glasshouses have showrooms that are located on three or four floors and each floor may house a display of several thousand items. Many of the glassworks have remained in the ownership of the same families for hundreds of years, with many of their early works displayed in the local museum on Murano. Bowls, plates, and dishes using mosaic and millefiori pieces were made by Giavanni Barovier, circa 1860, and can be seen on display in the museum. Sadly for the paperweight collector, the museum does not have one antique paperweight on show, although they do display a few millefiori canes and several portrait head canes.

Collecting the Cullet.
The island of Murano is serviced by a fleet of ferries and small barges; here the collection of cullet is loaded for removal to the mainland. Many of the glassworks are located directly on the canal side and occasionally, during routine dredging to stop the canals from silting up, choice items of glass are found intact, thrown directly into the canal by a worker not happy with the slight flaw he can see in the glass.

Shopping Murano Style.
The island of Murano has a charm that entices glass collectors from all over the world. Although paperweights with a Made in Murano label have not always been regarded in the highest esteem by serious collectors of weights, the pretty houses, canal-side walks, and the emergence of paperweights that are now beginning to be taken seriously by collectors should make this holiday destination a must for all who have not already visited Murano.

Typical Murano Glassworks.
As you walk around Murano looking in the dozens of shops all selling glassware, there are many alleyways between the buildings that entice the curious visitor with small signs that tell you that there is yet another glassworks hidden behind the shopfronts. At present there are approximately 150 glasshouses on Murano and many like this one may be a small concern of five or six men or you could open the door to a substantial producer employing many hundreds of workers.

Calle Corte Bigaglia.
High on the wall with the peeling paint is the sign for Calle Corte Bigaglia, so named in honor of Pietro Bigaglia (1786-1876) who has been credited with the manufacture of the first true paperweight. He exhibited paper-weights as early as 1845 in Vienna and won a prize medal for the quality of his wares, but to have reached this stage of excellence, he must have made weights for a considerable time prior to this exhibition. The alleyway leads to a small enclosed courtyard with trees and a glassworks at the far end. It was not possible to establish if the glassworks had been connected to Bigaglia in the nineteenth century during my short stay on the island, but it would seem likely that a connection exists.

Calle Corte Bigaglia.
It is quite possible that this is the original glassworks where Pietro Bigaglia constructed his first weights; but, unfortunately the works was closed on my short visit to Murano. The glassworks is still operational to this day and has not changed significantly in the last 150 years or so.

Window in Calle Corte Bigaglia.
This window is in a house at the entrance to Calle Corte Bigaglia and is of modern construction, but may be a modern day reference to the work carried out at the glassworks at the end of the courtyard. This spiral crown technique has been in use by the Venetian glassworkers for several hundred years.

Street scene on Murano.
Murano has an advantage over its neighbor Venice in that it is possible to walk around the fascinating and charming canals. Everyday life continues for the 3000 residents with most of the menfolk working in the substantial glassmaking factories; with the complete absence of the automobile the only noise comes from the small boats and the regular ferry to the mainland. The island offers many canal side restaurants and a museum of antique glass, all within a short walk of the ferry landings. I spent three days on Murano but am already planning a return visit to this enchanting island which allows you to step back to a leisurely way of life as experienced by the local inhabitants of one hundred and fifty years ago.

Filligree box with figure cane, c. 1850. Dia. 2". *Courtesy of Anne Anderson.* $1500/2000.

This is an extremely rare example of the type of work being produced in Venice around the 1850s. The central glass disc has a figure and aventurine encased with other glass canes to adorn this beautifully made silver filigree box which would have been an expensive item to produce, even in the mid-1800s. Items such as this box and the following scent bottles were bought as souvenirs and gifts by the travelers and tourists of the time on the Grand Tour.

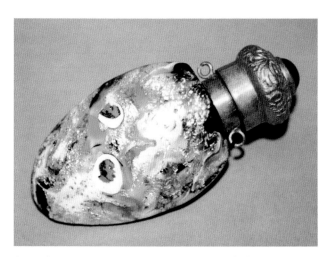

Scent bottle with Negro portrait canes, c. 1850. Length 2.75". *Courtesy of Roy and Pam Brown.* $800/1500.

The attribution of the scent bottles and other objects with portrait canes is best left to the persons who have studied them in great detail as it would appear that three or four people, as well as G. B. and G. Franchini, were making the portrait canes from the 1850s to the later part of the nineteenth century. Among those known to be making portraits were the father and son team of Vincenzo Moretti (1835-1901) and Luigi Moretti (1867-1946). A book that covers the attribution and manufacture of glass canes and the objects into which they were inserted during the nineteenth century, was written by Giavanni Sarpellon and published in 1990 by Prestel Books, New York, USA. Sarpellon is the recognized leading authority on the subject and a noted collector of mosaic glass. The book pays particular attention to pieces that have the portraits of Italian national heroes and landmarks from the Venetian region and will delight the collector of Venetian glass and paperweights alike.

Scent bottle with white birds, c. 1850. Length 2.75". *Courtesy of Roy and Pam Brown.* $800/1500.

The white birds on this scent bottle are made in the same way as portrait canes. Each part of the bird is made from segments of different colored glass and assembled like a mosaic. As each piece is carefully added to build up the picture, they are fused together at the lamp before being heated up to the point where the cane can be drawn out to several feet in length. The cane is then cut into small segments of less than a quarter inch thickness, retaining the motif throughout the whole length of the rod.

Scent bottle, c. 1850. Length 2.75". *Courtesy of Roy and Pam Brown.* $700/1000.
This scent bottle has retained the original gold chain that enabled the bottle to be worn around the neck and used whenever required. Perfumes were used widely in the nineteenth century to ward off the obnoxious smells of the street and the unwashed. Perfume and deodorant were used by the Romans several thousand years ago and some of the earliest glass vials and containers were used to carry these materials. Many early Roman bottles have very small apertures to dispense the very expensive perfume sparingly. This scent bottle has been signed Venize and was certainly bought as a memento of a visit to this beautiful city on the route of the Grand Tour.

Scent bottle with four portrait canes, c. 1850. Length 2.75". *Courtesy of Roy and Pam Brown.* $1000/1500.
This scent bottle has four portrait canes which appear to be one male and three of the same female heads. The heads are set upon a green and aventurine ground with a very ornate collar to the neck of the bottle. The stopper is attached to the collar with a fine safety chain and is in pristine condition.

Scent bottle with a molded top, c. 1850. Length 2.75". *Courtesy of Margaret Preston.* $1000/1500.
This scent bottle also has a cane with a gondola in it plus two portrait canes. The top is not as fine as the previous piece but is still sought after by collectors.

Paperknife, seal, and scent bottle, c. 1850. *Courtesy of Roy and Pam Brown and Margaret Preston.*
Many uses for decorative millefiori canes were found by the Venetians as can be seen by this grouping of beautifully preserved items. Many items such as cane handles were not quite up to the rigors of everyday use and unfortunately many that have survived show chips, bruises, and fractures.

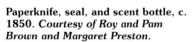

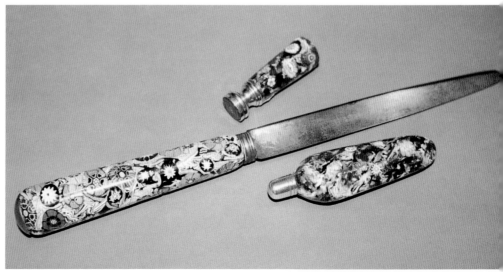

Close up of a cane handle, c. 1850. Length 2.75". *Author's collection*. $600/750.
The gondola cane seen in this handle was made by the Franchini family and is set among other complex millefiori canes. These items were quite expensive to produce and were bought by the rich and nobility of the nineteenth century, and often bound with the finest of materials. In this piece the band at the base of the glass is solid gold.

Left:
Close up of cane handle.
This photo shows a lovely rose cane in pink with a garland of star dust canes. The rose petals are made very finely, similar to the French Clichy version of a rose that was produced just after this rose. The use of aventurine in most millefiori pieces is indicative of the market these items were aimed at as this material was expensive to make and used very sparingly.

Side view of Franchini scrambled paperweight.
The paperweight has a very low profile and measures only one and three eighths inches high.

Franchini scrambled paperweight, c. 1850. Dia 2.5", Height 1.375". *Author's collection*. $500/750.
In this paperweight, a checker board cane can be seen with other white on blue canes that look as though they should be representative of something, but I have not worked out what. This weight has many pieces of ribbon and latticinio canes and patches of aventurine. A common feature of many of these early paperweights is the lack of a smooth dome of glass to enhance the canework. The canes are almost to the surface of the weight, which has a slightly unfinished look and feel. The outer covering of glass has an orange peel look, as though it requires another heating and smoothing by the glassworker. The whole canes look to be reasonably well spaced and set meaningfully and it may be that this is one of the very earliest of weights to have been made in Venice. The weight is not even perfectly round and is slightly oval.

Base view of Franchini scrambled paperweight.
A typical base of these early weights shows a broken pontil mark and quite heavy wear to the basal ring although the weight pivots on the pontil mark; again, little thought has gone into the construction of the weight.

Scrambled Franchini paperweight, c. 1850. Dia. 2.75", Height 1.375". *Courtesy of a private collector.* **$500/750.**
Long lengths of spiral, twisted, and latticinio canes make this an attractive weight. There are no millefiori or even broken fragments at all in this weight, which has a smoother, more finished look to it than the previous example.

Swirl Paperweight/Witches Ball, c. 1850. Dia. 2.7", Height 1.7". *Courtesy of Margaret Preston.* **$300/500.**
This swirl weight is typical of the early and later Murano paperweights. The style has changed little in one hundred and fifty years. This piece has a hole at the bottom about half an inch in diameter. These have been recorded from Bohemia as well as Italy. Although it may look like a paperweight, it would not be stable enough to hold down paper and has been suggested that they were displayed on a pole in the garden as ornamental.

Side view of Franchini paperweight.
The side view shows the low profile of this early weight, which also has the broken unground pontil mark.

Glass platter, nineteenth century. Dia. 9". *Author's collection.* **$600/800.**
This is a fine example of latticinio work and spiral canes. The center of the platter would make a superb swirl weight. This piece was made around the later part of the nineteenth century.

Small glasshouse and showroom on Murano.
Murano has approximately one hundred and fifty working glasshouses, and the glass lover can get access to most of them. This photograph shows a typical small works where the visitor is welcome to walk in off the street and watch the glass being worked. In this small unit, the visitor can browse among shelves of paperweights and all manner of glass objects at leisure with no pressure to buy. Usually a shop assistant is on hand to answer any questions you may wish to ask of the workmen.

Bags of millefiori canes.
Of the many glasshouses on Murano it would appear that only three or four actually make canes. All the other factories buy from these sources, which means that most paperweights coming from Murano look and appear to be from the same glassworks. When a paperweight has a sticker on the base saying it was Made in Murano it is impossible to tell from which glassworks it came. Very occasionally a paperweight will have a factory name, but these are very few and far between. Only by buying directly from the glassworks door can the firm be reliably identified. The shops on the mainland and Venice only sell weights with the Made in Murano sticker, so if you do visit and wish to know the maker, buy direct on Murano.

Murano Glassworkers.
The Muranese glassworkers are so used to having visitors in the workplace, it is possible to get in really close to see just how they do it

Through a shop window.
Canes as big as doorstops can be found in Murano at a price of around $110 for the cane on the left of the photo and the small mementos from around two or three dollars each.

Murano weights on display.
The numbers of paperweights on show is quite staggering. The totals available to buy must run to many thousands, with the quality ranging from very poor to some quite superb weights with prices to match. These weights were around four inches in diameter and priced around $150 each. I got the impression, while on Murano, that the bigger the weight, the higher the price tag, with little thought as to the quality aspect. With just a few exceptions, the weights are mass produced by the thousands with little variation in design by each glasshouse.

Giant Paperweight.
The only word to describe this weight is "enormous." It measures twelve inches in diameter and six inches in height. The piece was probably made for a center piece or exhibition. Although enormous in size and beautifully finished, the cane work lacks the precision this piece deserves.

Paperweight door handles. $150.
This door handle pair is very well made in the style of a four color crown weight and would not look out of place in any collector's home.

Fish Bowls. Dia. 9", Height 9".
These round fish bowls are made at many glasshouses on Murano. These were made by the A. V. Mazzega company and, although they do not put a price label on the pieces, they are for sale with a price of approximately $800/1000.

Fish tank. Height 15", Length 22".
This is a complete fish tank with no maintenance, feeding problems, or asking the neighbors to keep an eye on them while on vacation. Made by the Mazzega company, the fish are very well modeled at the lamp with the added attraction of sea weed and air bubbles. The tank is made as a slab four or five inches thick.

Assorted fish bowls.
The showrooms of the Mazzega company had many different types and sizes of fish tanks to suit everyone's taste. The lampwork was of a quite high standard in these pieces and the variety of choice in bowls or tanks was enormous.

Typical showroom display.
There are dozens of small showrooms on Murano and in Venice, all selling the production of Murano glasshouses. Some of the items are well made and tasteful, but the majority are of the mass produced variety.

Murano ring tray.
Popular items on display in many shops are the glass rings with central millefiori cane. The canes are set into various grounds with many containing aventurine.

Tray of millefiori brooches. From $15 to $45.
This tray of brooches shows that Murano products can be very well made with a very precise setting to the canes and motifs. With such vast amounts of millefiori cane being produced, most of the products are very realistically priced to ensure a sale to the millions of visitors that are attracted to this special part of the world.

Murano millefiori platter. Dia. 12". *Author's collection*. $550.
This was a piece I bought as my souvenir of Murano. It is well made with canes that are all the same size and in a great variety of colors and shapes. The platter is precisely made and one of the best I saw while on Murano. The quality and prices can vary quite dramatically as can be seen in the next piece.

Murano platter. Dia. 12". $580.
The quality of this scattered end of day piece does not compare to the previous platter. The edges of this piece are very uneven, as though it had been rolled out like a piece of dough. There are many broken canes in the design and for the price of 1,080.000 lira I would prefer the previous piece, which was more reasonably priced.

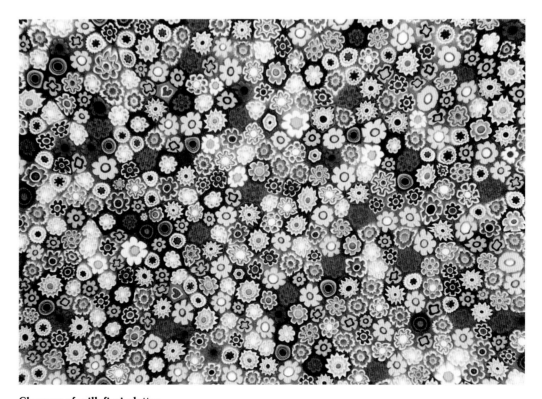

Close up of millefiori platter.
This close up shows a good variety of canes and is always useful as a reference piece to identify other Murano pieces.

Chinese weights on Murano. With the many thousands of paperweights to choose from on Murano, you would have thought that it would be inappropriate to import Chinese paperweights into Murano for fear that it could damage this already very competitive area of the gifts trade; but, several shops that I visited had on display many of these cheap imports. The prices were much lower than the local produce and not one weight had any distinguishing marks to say it had been Made in China. The prices started at $8 for a typical anemone to $20 for a patterned millefiori weight.

Vetreria concentric millefiori paperweight. Dia. 3.5", Height 2".
This and several of the following weights were shown to me by the Vetreria showroom manager when I asked if there were any quality collectors paperweights being made on Murano at the present time. He brought out this beautiful concentric which he said had been made as a test piece by the company's most experienced glassmaker, named Bruno. The quality of the glass and cane sizing were a match for any modern paperweight, but the paperweight proved to be too expensive to produce in quantity for the collector markets and the project was dropped. He went on to say that the price for the weight would be about $500.

Side view of Vetreria paperweight.
The traditional way of identifying paperweights made on Murano was to look in profile at the ends of the canes which would usually show varying lengths and look similar to a profile of the Rocky Mountains; but, the maker of this weight has recognized that care needs to be taken when cutting lengths of cane. This weight shows a perfect profile.

Franco Schiavon Water Lily paperweight. Dia. 3", Height 2".
This paperweight was made at the glasshouse of Franco Schiavon as a test piece and has not been sold onto the market as yet. This and several others were shown to me as weights that were being considered for export by a distributor of Murano products. If they ever go into production, I am sure they will meet with approval from the serious paperweight collector. Prices for these pieces were not available.

Franco Schiavon fancy cut paperweight with flower and garland. Dia. 3", Height 3.75".
This weight is cut with many side facets that give an interesting look to this garlanded piece. Many early twentieth century weights originate from eastern Europe with this multifaceted shape. Hungary and Czechoslovakia are currently making this type of weight and it could easily be mistaken for a paperweight produced in the 1920/30 period. No prices were available.

**Franco Schiavon Lampworked Bouquet.
Dia. 2.75", Height 2.2".**
This lovely example has been flashed over with royal blue and then faceted to reveal the motif. Five different flowers, including a viola and pansy with two butterflies with millefiori wings, can be seen within the interior of the weight. The lampwork has been meticulously assembled and is a real collector's piece. No prices were available.

Franco Schiavon display platter. Height 12".
This platter is signed with an M near the base of the stem, which I was told meant Murano; but, it could be the glassworker's own signature as there was a little language problem during the interviews with the sales people. The piece pivots on a stand and the canes are set into a matt black glass to great effect. No prices were available.

Murano close packed millefiori paperweight. Dia. 3.5", Height 2".
Author's collection. $150/250.
This is a nice example of a close packed weight that was probably made around the 1980s and has a nice representative selection of canes from Murano. I suppose that at some later point in time it would be possible to get the cane factories identified, although with the price of Murano weights low in comparison to most other manufacturers of paperweights, it would not be a cost effective exercise until Murano weights are collected seriously and are appreciating significantly in value.

Murano scrambled paperweight. Dia. 2.8", Height 1.75".
Courtesy of Gary and Marge McClanahan. $125/150.
Made at the end of the day or by the apprentices, this type of weight has been made by virtually every glassworks that made paperweights.

Murano scrambled paperweight, c. 1950. Dia. 2.75", Height 1.8". ***Courtesy of Gary and Marge McClanahan. $150/175.***
This is a well made weight but of an indeterminable age. From the early 1950s, this and most other weights we see on the general market were made in great abundance. Unless the paperweight has a yellow cast to the glass, which would signify that it was made from around 1930 to 1950, then we have to assume that it was made in the second half of the twentieth century. Very few weights were made in Murano that were reliably dated. Many weights attributed with nineteenth century dates have been found to be spurious.

Murano scrambled paperweight. Dia. 2.9", Height 1.8". ***Courtesy of Gary and Marge McClanahan. $60/100***
This version has used much larger canes and can still be found in abundance in Murano today. It was a perfect way to dispose of waste cane and glass and still make a profit.

29

Murano Marguerite over latticinio. Dia. 3", Height 2". *Courtesy of Gary and Marge McClanahan.* **$200/300.**
Another paperweight with well made flowers over latticinio, but this piece is lacking quality in the final stage of assembly with the leaves adrift from the stem and disturbance in the latticinio strands. Probably all due to the pressure of meeting output targets, it would only take a few extra minutes on each weight to enhance the product by 100%. It appears that the leaves have been stretched and pulled while in contact with the latticinio, whereas the leaves should be made separately and then placed on to the motif.

Murano flower posy over latticinio. Dia. 3", Height 2". *Courtesy of Gary and Marge McClanahan.* **$200/250.**
A very pretty display of millefiori canes set out as flower heads. The canes are extremely well made with Clichy type pastry molds and others that have been selected in this fantasy flower set up to represent no particular flower, but a mixture of flowers that clothe the meadow. Some of the canes are of particular interest, such as the buttercup yellow cane and the pink cane near the center which are of a particularly fine nature. These canes are quite common in Murano weights but are usually found in concentrics, which is not to their best advantage. In this design and other spaced millefiori weights, the canes can be seen at their best. The leaves and canes are set directly on the latticinio bed, which has resulted in a little movement of the strands.

Side view of Murano flower posy over latticinio.
In this view it is possible to see just how close the motif is to the top of the weight. As the set up almost covers the top of the weight, it has not been necessary to encase the weight with a large dome of glass for its magnifying properties.

Murano three flower paperweight. Dia. 3", Height 2". *Courtesy of Gary and Marge McClanahan.* **$200/300.**
The flower motifs made on Murano are almost limitless in variety and colors and although great skills are needed to produce these weights, very few come up to the quality demanded by collectors. It is a great way to get started on the paperweight collecting trail, as a wide variety of styles are available at budget prices; however, collectors soon move on to finer quality products. The three flowers in this weight would have taken considerable time and skill to make and would be good enough to get into all but the most exclusive of collections.

Murano bluebirds paperweight. Dia. 3", Height 2". *Courtesy of Gary and Marge McClanahan.* **$300/350.**
Since around 1980, the quality of the Muranese paperweight has increased dramatically without being aimed at the quality collector market, but occasionally weights like this pair of bluebirds do actually achieve collector status. These birds are standing on a realistic green and earth ground similar to the Baccarat antique rock grounds and would be a welcome addition to most collections. The better quality weights would seem to be targeted at the USA as hardly any appear in the UK.

Murano all over faceted paperweight. Dia. 3", Height 2.5". *Courtesy of Gary and Marge McClanahan.* **$400/600.**
Fine and precise faceting gives this weight collectibility. The central motif of flower heads and small stems with leaves are packed in tightly over a well made latticinio basket. The motif is then multiplied by the all-over facets which make this piece desirable and quite rare. After visiting thirty retail shops during my visit to Murano in February 2000, it was almost impossible to find weights of this quality on sale.

Murano basket paperweight. Dia. 3", Height 2". *Courtesy of Gary and Marge McClanahan.* **$450/600.**
This is an extremely fine and rare basket with torsade and handle, for a weight made in Murano. This paperweight oozes quality and is a credit to the unknown worker who made it, The glass is of a clear crystal with six side and a large top facet to view the basket inside. The flowers within the basket are finely crafted with greenery to fill out the spaces. Much care and attention has gone into the production of this weight. It was possibly a test piece.

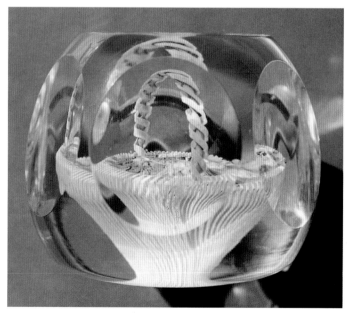

Side view of Murano basket paperweight.
A beautifully made handle stretches gracefully over the basket with the handle made from a double twist of pink and white cable and attached delicately to the basket without disturbing the latticinio which makes up the very fine basket that tapers down to the flat base.

Murano silhouette paperweight. Dia. 3.3", Height 2.25". *Courtesy of Gary and Marge McClanahan.* **$80/100.**

A silhouette of a rooster centers this gift weight from Murano. The tell-tale uneven canes around the periphery inform you this weight was made on the island of Murano, even without a paper label stuck to the base. Specifically aimed at the millions of tourists who visit Murano and Venice every year, the price of around $80 puts it within reach of all visitors as a memento of their visit.

Murano concentric with torsade. Dia. 3", Height 2.7". *Courtesy of Gary and Marge McClanahan.* **$400/600.**

A fine concentric with a closely spun latticinio torsade in milky white glass. The set up of the canes is almost flawless. This is a beautifully crafted paperweight of the highest caliber. If the weight had been an antique St. Louis, it would have commanded a price of ten times the value of this lovely piece.

Murano close packed paperweight. Dia. 3", Height 2.25". *Courtesy of Gary and Marge McClanahan.* **$150/200.**

This is a nicely designed weight, with open millefiori canes with interesting and varied centers. Packed tightly together with no slippage, it is reminiscent of the antique Baccarat bouquet de marriage designed to resemble a bride's bouquet. The outer part of each cane is made from a circle of tiny white rods. Although the cane looks as though it is hollow, it is in fact filled with clear glass.

Side view of Murano concentric with torsade.

The weight has a very high dome of glass over the canes to enhance the view with the torsade floating just off the base. The base is always ground flat on Murano weights and the central canes are drawn down to the base as in a mushroom weight to finish off very neatly.

Murano seven row concentric paperweight. Dia. 3.25", Height. 2.6". *Courtesy of Gary and Marge McClanahan.* $100/150.
Tightly packed canes in a nice gift weight that can be found at most antique malls and fairs — a good value for the money but not of a high collectible standard. Most new collectors start by acquiring Murano weights such as this piece, which usually remains in the collection as too good to trade or give away.

Murano dated 1846 paperweight. Dia. 3", Height 2.2". *Author's collection.* $60/80.
This is a poorly made carpet ground weight which has loosely packed canes of a simple construction. It is dated 1846 and the glass has a very slight yellow tinge. The date is spurious and it has been recorded by visitors to glassworks on Murano in the 1950/60 era, that dated weights were made to order and practically any date could be inserted at only a little extra cost. Dated paperweights from Murano are not too common, but the workmanship in most of these weights means they are relatively easy to spot as not from the classic period of 1845 to 1852 when most English and French antique weights were produced.

Murano Marbrie and millefiori paperweight. Dia. 3.25", Height 2.25". *Courtesy of Gary and Marge McClanahan.* $400/600.
Marbrie weights are very rare and difficult to create; but, the glassworker has managed to include a miniature five row concentric into this design as a bonus. The skill levels of the paperweight makers of Murano can be of the highest standard, but can also be unbelievably poor. This weight has been faceted on four sides and the top with deeply cut indents between the facets. The millefiori set up is also well done in neat rings of colorful but simple canes.

Murano dated 1852 millefiori and twist paperweight. Dia. 3", Height 2". *Courtesy of Terry and Hilary Johnson.* $100/150.
Packed flowers are set over a green ground of melted chipping's, with strands of twisted pink and white ribbon separating the flower canes. A devil and a spurious date of 1852 on a white ground add interest, but the unwary are easily caught out by these fake dates.

33

Murano basket of flowers with 1848 date cane. Dia. 3", Height 2.1". *Courtesy of Terry and Hilary Johnson. $150/175.*
This is a nice modern paperweight from the island of Murano. It stands out from most of the gift weights bought in abundance by the many visitors to Italy. It is made and designed with care and this paperweight is worth the guide price of $150 plus. The trouble with the spurious dated weights is that they end up on the secondary market where people can get caught by an unknowledgeable vendor in all things old and if the purchase is made abroad, then the chance of recovering the money paid, on realization that the weight is not an antique, is highly unlikely. As long as this guide price is not exceeded by much, then this weight is a nice decorative object for the sideboard.

Close up of dated 1848 Murano paperweight.
The flowers are quite well made and are set above a ground of white lace with the date cane standing out clearly on a white plaque.

Right:
Fratelli Toso millefiori canes used c. 1960 up to c. 1980. *Courtesy of a private collector.*
This page shows a wide selection of simple and very complex canes including roses. The cane makers have completed their part of the product in some style, but the majority of these canes have ended up in paperweights that do not match the quality of the canes.

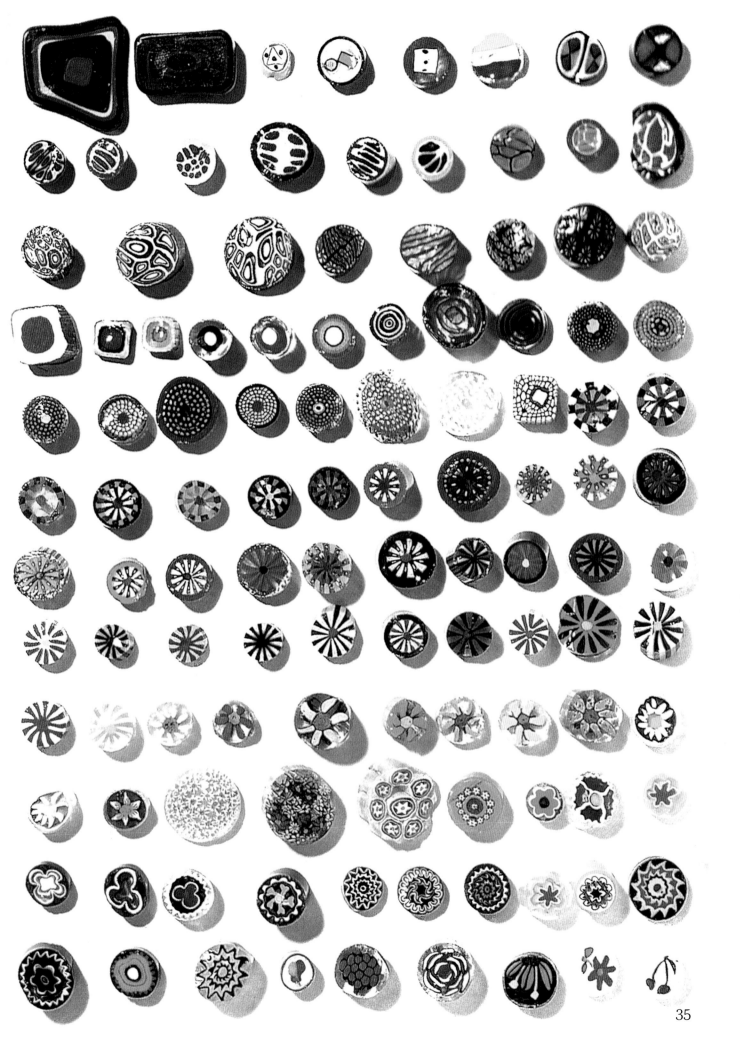

Bohemian Paperweights

Bohemia could be credited as the possible birthplace of millefiori paperweights in the form and content that we know today. Millefiori canes were used before 1840 in glasses, bowls, and other vessels, including a bottle that can be seen in the Metropolitan Museum of Art and illustrated in Paul Hollister's *Encyclopaedia of Glass Paperweights*, page 27. The canes in this bottle show the same composition and styles as most of the following Bohemian examples. This bottle is attributed to Franz Pohl (1813-84) and was probably made around 1835/40. Pohl is also known to have worked at the Josephine Glassworks in 1841 and canes very similar to those used in the bottle are found in paperweights. The Bohemian glassmakers have a history of fine glassmaking that reaches far into the distant past, with the Riesengebirge in the north of Czechoslovakia being one of the main glass producing areas. Some millefiori paperweights are dated, with the earliest being 1848. Occasionally, these paperweights include a lower case j set above the date in the same way Baccarat signed and dated their weights, although the Baccarat B is in capitals. It is thought that this j represents the Josephine Glassworks, which was established in 1841 and who in 1844 had produced trade catalogues which showed millefiori items.

Antique Bohemian millefiori paperweights and glassware are on a par with the finest examples made by the French makers of the same period; but, the Bohemians excelled in the production of overlay glass. Many vases were made with paperweight bases that had the vase body overlaid with another color, which was then fancy cut to decorate the piece. Millefiori paperweights were also overlaid, with windows cut to view the interior motif. Many of these Bohemian paperweights may also feature silhouette canes of animals and human figures which adds extra interest. These silhouettes are sometimes found as a large single element in a rod but can also be a tiny central part of a cane and can only be seen under a strong magnifying glass.

The antique weights made in Bohemia are different from their French counterparts in that the glass is a composition of lime, potash and soda which gives the weight a much lighter feel than a French paperweight which has a high lead content. Other differences can be seen in the illustrated examples following this introduction. There is also a distinct difference between the finer paperweights attributed to Bohemia and the less well made. The gap in workmanship is obvious for all to see and would also seem to indicate that the finer weights originated from the same glassworks and with the others being made by possibly two or three other manufacturers, most probably all in the same area. If we assume that the Josephine Glassworks produced the finest pieces, we then have around 60 or so other glassworks to choose from that could have made the rest of these slightly different antique paperweights. Detailed examination of the histories of these other glassworks may reveal the identity of the makers of these slightly inferior weights in the future.

Czechoslovakia still produces fine crystal in huge quantities that is exported worldwide, often with a label stating *Bohemian Glass*. Today, paperweights are made throughout this part of Europe, using many of the lampwork and millefiori styles of the past, but so far none have managed to match the skill of the glassmakers of antiquity.

Bohemian signed and dated 1848 spaced paperweight. Dia. 2.8". *Courtesy of Karen and Paul Dunlop. Photo ©2000 Papier Presse. $2,000/4,000.*
This first Bohemian paperweight demonstrates the immense variety of silhouette canes that can be found in these weights. Close examination will reveal a multitude of butterflies, running rabbits, eagles, horses, dogs, and a date cane with the lower case j over 1848. I have never seen so many silhouettes within one paperweight. I counted seventeen, but there may be more that I cannot see on the photograph I have.

Bohemian close packed millefiori paperweight, c. 1850. Dia. 3".
Author's collection. $1,500/2,500.
This paperweight is faceted all over with thumbnail cuts and a large top window. This weight could easily be mistaken for a Baccarat piece, but although the close pack canes are almost identical to a Baccarat close pack in terms of setting and coloring, the weight is very light when compared to a similar Baccarat piece. This weight has a row of various colored arrowhead canes grouped around the central cane which are also very similar to antique Baccarat weights. The antique Bohemian close packed paperweights are much rarer than the French equivalents.

Base view of Bohemian close packed millefiori paperweight.
The base is very typical of Bohemian weights. In almost all cases the bases are left flat, which allows the glass to become very scratched and in some examples the base may look like a modern matte finished Chinese paperweight. The canes in this example are drawn together and finished with a slight twist. The pontil mark is removed by grinding of the base, but occasionally a dimple is ground where the pontil was.

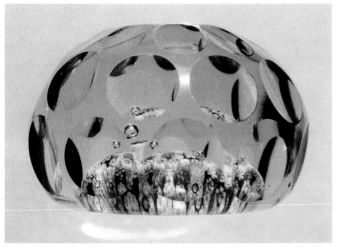

Side view of Bohemian close packed millefiori paperweight.
The side view reveals the set up of canes placed low down near the base whereas the Baccarat equivalent would be set higher up in the dome and would look from above as if the whole dome of glass was stuffed full of canes.

**Bohemian spaced millefiori paperweight, c. 1850. Dia. 2.8",
Height 1.5".** *Author's collection.* **$700/1,000.**
This almost looks like an end of day weight, because of the placement of
split and broken canes in between the whole canes in the two concentric
rows. The canes are six, seven, and eight segments around a central cane
made in the same way. The central cane is also similar in style and size to
the rest of the other canes, a larger central cane would have given much
more appeal to the weight.

**Bohemian spaced millefiori on latticinio, c. 1850. Dia. 2.9",
Height 1.5".** *Courtesy of Gary and Marge McClanahan.* **$700/900.**
Pure white latticinio, or lace as it is sometimes called, highlights the colorful
selection of canes set around the red Devil cane in the center. The strongly
colored canes all follow the same format of six, seven, eight, or nine small
cog canes set around a single small cog cane, which in this weight is a small
component of the other canes.

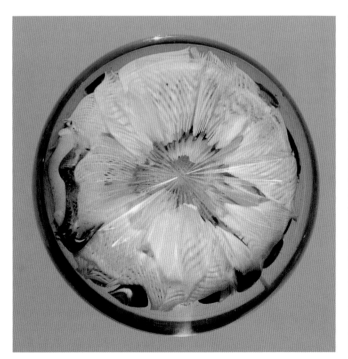

Base of Bohemian spaced millefiori paperweight.
The base view reveals a bed of latticinio canes for the featured canes to
rest upon. The rather flat base has been finished with a precise star cutting
across the base. This star cutting gets rid of the pontil mark and adds
interest to the base.

**Bohemian two row concentric millefiori paperweight, c. 1850.
Dia. 2.7", Height 1.7".** *Courtesy of Gary and Marge McClanahan.*
$1,000/1,500.
A good selection of canes are spaced around the central feature cane with
a red devil. This cane is also sometimes referred to as a running monkey.
The complex canes are set on a bed of latticinio. The variously colored
canes are seen through a flat window ground into the top of the weight.

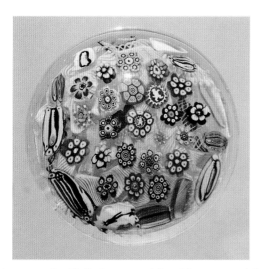

Bohemian spaced millefiori paperweight with pansy and flower canes, c. 1850. Dia. 2.75", Height 1.5". *Author's collection.* **$1,000/1,500.**

The same devil or monkey figure can be seen in two canes. The larger figure in white is set on a blue ground and the same silhouette rod is in the central cane but only as the central component of the cane, as if the artisan who created this piece had hidden it and was inviting closer inspection to find the silhouettes. This weight also displays several varieties of arrow canes, with part of the sharp end of the arrow missing. In other canes, the whole arrowhead can be seen. These arrow canes are also called anchor canes and often have a rounded shape as in a ship's anchor. The cane at seven o clock is designed as a pansy cane. This cane comprises four pale blue arrow rods set above two larger lower petals with anchors, and with all six elements set around a red and white center. Other flowers can be seen at two o clock and eleven o clock, the former comprising six white on red petals and the latter five white on green petals. Discovering these flower elements in paperweights from Bohemia is fascinating and exciting, as you never know what will turn up once you look in greater detail with a magnifying glass. In some weights, the figures can be as small as a pin head, usually as the center of a larger cane. I suggest you all get out your Bohemian weights and have another look.

Bohemian spaced paperweight. Dia. 3", Height 1.5". *Author's collection.* **$1,000/1,500.**

This paperweight has a good variety of canes but without the figure or flower types. What it lacks in complex canes, it makes up for in the lovely bed of latticinio the canes rest upon. In this specimen we can see that the white latticinio is interspersed with pink spiral canes which give the ground a rose hue. Four arrow or anchor canes in dark blue on white are set around the larger center cane.

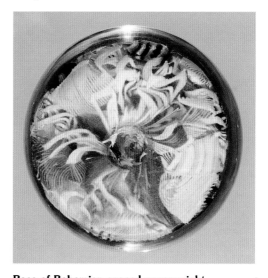

Base of Bohemian spaced paperweight.
The base clearly shows the spiral canes and the small dimple mark where the pontil has been removed.

Bohemian spaced millefiori with nosegay and flower canes, c. 1850. Dia. 3", Height 1.6". *Private collection.* **$2,750.**

This very fine spaced millefiori weight, has a wonderful selection of un-usual millefiori canes to keep you looking. The central cane is unusually large and centers the weight nicely. The lovely selection of figure and flower canes are spaced evenly over the surface of this paperweight with a high degree of skill. Among the feature canes to be found are four white on blue monkey or devil figures, singularly or as the tiny center element of a complex cane, a very rare nosegay cane can be viewed at the one o clock position, and other very fine canes, obviously designed to represent flow-ers. Cast your eyes over this lovely and special paperweight and see if you can spot the flowers.

Bohemian spaced millefiori on latticinio paperweight, c. 1850. Dia. 2.75". *Courtesy of Karen and Paul Dunlop. Photo ©2000 Papier Presse.* **$1,200/1,500.**

A remarkable dog silhouette centers this lovely and tightly packed, spaced millefiori paperweight. The central cane has a white dog on a dark ground which has nine individual elements surrounding it which have then been encased in a white and dark ruby glass tube. Several other canes are also encased in this tube-like structure. Several of the canes show a slight variation from the normal Bohemian canes usually made with six, seven, and eight stars and cogs around a central core. In this weight we can see that the simple elementary canes are them-selves surrounded by star dust and cog canes, which gives each of these canes a much more complex and sophisticated look.

Bohemian spaced concentric over filigree canes, c. 1850. Dia. 2.75". *Courtesy of Karen and Paul Dunlop. Photo ©2000 Papier Presse.* **$2,000/3,000.**
A long legged poodle type of dog silhouette centers this beautifully made weight. The set up rests above a bed of spiraling white filigree canes which makes the paperweight much rarer than the usual paperweights set above a bed of latticinio.

Bohemian crown paperweight, c. 1850. Dia. 2.9". *Courtesy of Karen and Paul Dunlop. Photo ©2000 Papier Presse.* **$4,000/5,000.**
A very rare and beautiful crown paperweight made from blue and white rods that radiate from a complex central cane to the base.

Side view of Bohemian crown paperweight.
The blue and white rods are drawn down to a flat base.

Bohemian red and white overlay, concentric mushroom paperweight, c. 1850. Dia. 3". *Courtesy of Karen and Paul Dunlop. Photo ©2000 Papier Presse.* **$5,000/6,000.**
Five concentric rows of pink, blue, and white colored complex canes are all set around the precisely located center cane in this stunning paperweight from Bohemia. A casual glance may have indicated a paperweight made by the Saint Louis or Baccarat glasshouses of France, but on closer inspection we realize that the millefiori canes are made with the same groupings of six or seven small canes set around another small cane that we have seen in many of the previous examples from Bohemia. This overlay paperweight demonstrates the heights reached by the Bohemian craftsmen in their quest for excellence.

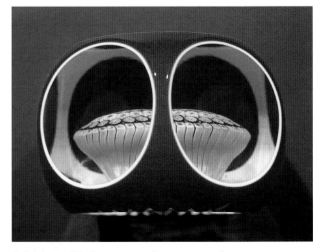

Side view of Bohemian overlay paperweight.
The white inner covering of glass can clearly be seen within the paperweight. The very neat outer row of white open tube canes are precisely drawn down to the base with a perfect degree of tapering to the mushroom stem. This very elegant stem is similar to the way the English glassworkers at Bacchus finished off their paperweights, with a row of hollow white tubes. The weight has very large facets cut to reveal the interior of the paperweight and the base is star cut right out to the edge of the paperweight sides.

Bohemian spaced paperweight with torsade, c. 1850. Dia. 2.5".
Courtesy of Karen and Paul Dunlop. Photo ©2000 Papier Presse.
$1,500/2,000.

Three monkey or devil canes are among the fine selection on view in this
special paperweight from Bohemia. A rose cane can be seen at 11 o'clock
that is similar to the famous Clichy rose. This rose has seven pink and white
sepals holding the inner pink petals together. Any paperweight with a rose
has added value, but when it is also encircled by a beautiful white torsade,
the paperweight becomes even more desirable to the collecting fraternity.

**Bohemian overlay vases with paperweight bases, c. 1850. Base
dia. 3", Height 8.6". *Courtesy of Karen and Paul Dunlop. Photo
©2000 Papier Presse.* $15,000/20,000 a pair.**

Magnificent overlay vases with the bonus of paperweight bases are the
ultimate in craftsmanship. The cutting on the vases is beautifully executed
with outstanding precision. The vases rest on a base that is constructed
with spaced millefiori canes over a lace ground of filigree rods.

Bohemian open concentric paperweight, c. 1850. Dia. 2.6".
Courtesy of Karen and Paul Dunlop. Photo ©2000 Papier Presse.
$1,000/1,200.

A central feature cane with a dark colored eagle on a white ground within
a ring of small cog canes makes this a good example of the cane maker's
art. Unusual canes such as this one should always be displayed in a prominent position as it adds so much interest to a paperweight. Apart from the
blue canes in the central area, the other canes are a slight departure from
most of the previously seen millefiori cane examples, in that these are open
cog and single complex canes.

**Bohemian lampworked pear paperweight, c. 1850. Dia. 2.5",
Height 1.6". *Courtesy of Margaret Preston.* $2,000/3,000.**

This is a very rare example of Bohemian lampwork as I have never before
seen this or any other examples of lampworked fruit. The pear is in two
shades of red and yellow and set over a clear ground with two rows of
Bohemian style canes. The pear is very well made but the millefiori canes
are placed quite loosely in two uneven circles which may indicate it originated from a different glassworks to the paperweights viewed so far in this
chapter, or that it was an experimental piece.

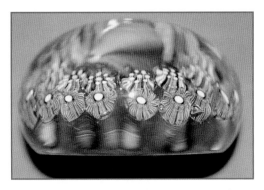

Side view of Bohemian lampworked pear paperweight.
The side view shows a low cushion-shaped glass dome with the fruit set high in the paperweight. The base is ground flat and striation can be seen in the glass. The canes around the pear are of the type normally found in paperweights attributed to this group of weights.

The paperweights we have viewed so far in this chapter have several things in common. First, most of the canes are constructed using small cane elements that are then set around another small element, to create a complex but simply made cane. Secondly, they are all well made and usually set out precisely with little or no slippage to the designs. The paperweights are very similar in design and construction and look very much alike. A conjectural view would be that these paperweights have probably been made at the Josephine Glassworks. The following examples do not look like the previous weights and are quite poorly made in most cases. They have probably been made in another glassworks, perhaps even in the same vicinity as the Josephine Glassworks but they do lack the precision that sets the earlier examples apart from this next batch. It is also likely that the following weights are not from the classic period, c. 1850, when quality was foremost, but made in a resurgence of interest in paperweights around the end of the nineteenth century.

Bohemian paperweight with roses. Dia. 2.8", Height 1.9". *Courtesy of a private collector.* **$500/750.**
This is a typical example in this group of paperweights of the slightly untidy placing of the canes that lacks the precision of the previous pieces. Gaps can be seen between each of the three concentric rows. The outer row is composed of very nice Clichy-type roses and even this row of prestige canes has gaps and displaced canes. With a little more care, the weight would have been worth twice as much as the value placed on it in this condition.

Bohemian miniature paperweight with white roses. Dia. 1.8", Height 1.3". *Courtesy of a private collector.* **$400/500.**
A tightly packed miniature with four white and green roses with pink and red millefiori centers. The canes are set around a royal blue complex cane with four odd blue canes in the outer row.

Bohemian paperweight with a pink rose. Dia. 2.3". *Courtesy of a private collector.* **$350/400.**
The two rows of complex green and yellow canes and blue and green canes are tightly set around a very nice pink rose with yellow stamens. The rose looks slightly crushed by the other canes and the set up is slightly off center.

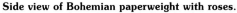

Bohemian paperweight with pink and white central rose. Dia. 2.8". *Courtesy of a private collector.* **$400/500.**
This weight has a garland of millefiori canes around the edge of the paperweight which has a peculiar white rose with red platelets that appears to have a piece missing. The other five green and white roses are complete but are poorly made in comparison to the Clichy variety.

Side view of Bohemian paperweight with roses.
The side view shows the set up high in the dome of the weight, with striations showing at the bottom of the glass. Bohemian classic paperweights rarely show striation in the glass. The outer row of canes show the well made roses set untidily, very close to the edge of the covering glass.

Bohemian miniature concentric with red rose. Dia. 1.8", Height 1.3". *Courtesy of a private collector.* **$350/450.**

The rose cane in the center of this miniature is the main feature and is quite well constructed, but does not stand out like a central feature should because the other canes are as large and very strongly colored. They are also set too close to the central cane.

Bohemian drawer pulls with rose canes. Height approx. 2". *Courtesy of a private collector.* **$400/600.**

A matching pair of drawer pulls that have two rows of canes, one with a mix of green and pink roses and candy colored canes. The inner row has pink and white pastry mold type canes. The pulls are set firmly in brass holding rings which are stamped with the name of TCJ ltd. BREVETTES.G.D on the collar.

Top view of drawer pull with rose canes.

The central white cane is constructed from twenty small complex canes to form this very impressive center piece. The pull does show evidence of striation, but in general it is a nice piece.

Bohemian patterned paperweight with white rose. Dia. 3", Height 1.9". *Courtesy of a private collector.* **$300/400.**

The pattern of lime green moss type canes are set over a clear ground around a concentric circle of red and blue complex canes which surround a green and white rose cane. The whole weight is spoiled due to the lack of harmony in the cane coloring.

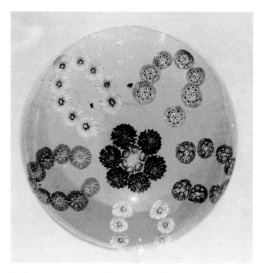

Bohemian patterned paperweight. Dia. 3.2", Height 2". *Author's collection.* **$250/350.**

The canes are set out in a C pattern around a central arrangement, but the weight has very little attractiveness in the coloring of the canes and it is also offset.

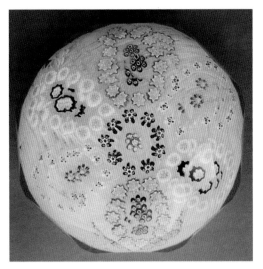

Earlier period Bohemian patterned paperweight, c. 1850 with facets. Dia. 3", Height 2". *Courtesy of Gary and Marge McClanahan.* **$1,000/1,500.**
I have placed this patterned paperweight on a bed of lace in this part of the chapter to show the obvious differences in the attention to detail shown by the craftsmen of the earlier period in paperweight production in Bohemia. In a difficult pattern to achieve, the canes are neatly set out in subtle colorings. This weight is also faceted all over. This weight is a credit to its makers and highly sought after by collectors.

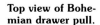

Drawer pull with lampworked flower. Dia. 2.1". *Author's collection.* **$500/750.**
The pull has been faceted all round the outer edge in this pretty lampworked flower which has several detached petals. The glass is a very clear crystal and is held in place by a brass collar.

Top view of Bohemian drawer pull.
The flower has several petals and a leaf detached which slightly detracts from its beauty. The petals have a cupped shape, which can be found in paperweights made around the 1930s.

Mounted paperweight. Dia. 1.7", Height 2.3". *Author's collection.* **$350/450.**
This paperweight with a stem similar to the drawer pulls is mounted on gilt metal work and set on a marble plaque. I have not quite decided what its use is, unless of course it is a paperweight adapted from a drawer pull. The paperweight part has been nicely made with complex canes.

Bohemian red flower. Dia. 2.8", Height 2.1". *Author's collection.* **$300/450.**
A red lampworked, six petal flower with four long slender leaves grows out of a spattered green ground made from chippings. The flower with a yellow center has smudges of detritus on the petals collected off the marver plate.

Bohemian four row concentric paperweight. Dia. 2.7", Height 1.8". *Courtesy of Terry and Hilary Johnson.* **$200/300.**
Four rows of tightly packed very complex canes give this weight a busy look. The central cane is very complex but is wasted when the rest of the paperweight is so sloppily made.

Bohemian close pack paperweight with rose and butterfly canes on mica ground, c. 1880. Dia. 2.7", Height 1.75". *Author's collection.* **$500/700.**
This paperweight can be reasonably dated until after the Paris World's Fair in 1878. The popularity for mica glass had been widely shown at this time and was then used extensively in Bohemian ornamental pieces. This type of mica paperweight must have been made in considerable numbers as they are regularly seen at auction in the US and Europe. The weight has several butterfly canes with the best seen at the 4 o'clock position and a rose cane at 10 o'clock. The weight has a good variety of canes, but none the same as the classic period, as seen in previous weights in this chapter.

Bohemian two row concentric paperweight. Dia. 2.5", Height 1.7". *Courtesy of a private collector.* **$400/500.**
This paperweight has been constructed with care and with a wonderful honeycomb cane in the center made from sixty individual parts. Honeycomb canes are very rare and add interest to the paperweight. This cane is made from tubes of pink with a white casing.

Side view of Bohemian red flower.
The flower sits on a very thin stem. The whole weight lacks the precision of a classic period paperweight and could have been made at any time after the turn of the twentieth century.

Bohemian five row concentric. Dia. 2.3", Height 1.6". *Courtesy of Terry and Hilary Johnson.* **$250/400.**
Tightly packed complex canes which have the look of a classic cane with small elements surrounding another small element, but the style is from the later period, c. 1920. The canes are pressed tightly together which helps to prevent slippage.

**Bohemian lampworked flowers. Dia. 2.8",
Height 1.9".** *Courtesy of Gary and Marge
McClanahan.* **$100/150.**
This paperweight has petals designed with upturned
edges and is loosely made over a spattered ground of
glass chippings. The lampwork flowers show little skill in
their creation.

**Bohemian lampworked flower over latticinio. Dia.
3", Height 2.1".** *Courtesy of Gary and Marge
McClanahan.* **$100/150.**
This paperweight highlights the skills that have been lost in
Bohemia since the classic period paperweights were made,
c. 1850. This flower has detached petals and a poorly
made net of white. Even as a mass produced gift weight,
the quality is very low.

Bohemian candlesticks. Diameter of base 3.5", Height 6.25".
Author's collection. **$600/700.**
A pair of well made candlesticks with a close packed paperweight base.
The candlesticks are faceted all over in a variety of cuts and they are
very heavy and stable.

Close up of candlestick base.
The canes are a selection of quite ordinary millefiori designs, mainly six
pointed cogs, encased in a variety of colors and then all set on a ground of
green mica. The cane colors are soft, almost pastel in shade, and lend little
to the appeal of the candlesticks — although this pair are used regularly for
their intended purpose in the author's dining room.

Bohemian flatware, c. 1850. *Courtesy of Karen and Paul Dunlop. Photo ©2000 Papier Presse.* **$1,500/2,000 per set.**
Beautiful table ware with matching handles in a mixture of mainly red, white, and blue colors, made from a superb selection of millefiori and spiral twist canes. The canes are a typical Bohemian mix but with several that are outstanding and rare. Flower canes can be found in all three pieces; but, in the knife and spoon a flower cane can be seen clearly with five arrowhead shaped petals on a small body with a stalk. The canes have been designed with care and interest in mind.

Bohemian paperweight, c. 1930. Dia. 3.25", Height 3". *Courtesy of Gary and Marge McClanahan.* **$150/250.**
This paperweight, which is faceted all over, is very typical and unmistakably from one of the dozens of glasshouses that were in operation in the northern part of Bohemia. They are usually very well made but with only simple lampworked flowers. Some do not have lampwork at all, the flowers being made from offcuts of canes that have been picked up from the marver plate and then encased within a glass dome. The paperweights from this area look very similar in design and have been copied by other countries in Europe and are still being made today. On a recent trip to Slovenia, in July 2000, a knowledgeable friend reported seeing as many as six of this type of paperweight in one antique shop alone, with a price of $60 each. It is extremely difficult to tell which are the antiques from c. 1900 and which were made yesterday, as they look so much alike. A more detailed explanation of the factories that were involved in paperweight production in this area may be found in Peter Von Brackel's book, *Paperweights, 1842 to Present*, Schiffer Publishing Ltd.

Bohemian paperweight, c. 1930. Dia. 3", Height 2.75".
Courtesy of Gary and Marge McClanahan. $150/200.
This paperweight has flowers made from round discs of multicolored glass which have been pierced by a steel pick while encased and still hot and pliable. This piercing forces down the central area of the flower to create the stem. Pink strands of glass fill in the base area.

Bohemian paperweight, c. 1930. Dia. 3", Height 2.75".
Courtesy of Gary and Marge McClanahan. $150/200.
A faceted and lampworked red and blue flower with green leaves over a white ground of glass chippings.

Bohemian paperweight, c. 1930. Dia. 3.25, Height 3". *Courtesy of Gary and Marge McClanahan. $150/250.*
A nice arrangement of flowers in this very colorful and decorative piece from Bohemia. It is possible that it could have been made at any time after the turn of the twentieth century. This weight has an arrangement of six small flowers set over a much larger, six petal flower which is then set above a red ground of melted glass chippings. The piece is faceted all over with a window on top. The base is flat ground with no pontil showing.

Bohemian sulphide lion. Dia. 2.9", Height 4".
Courtesy of Gary and Marge McClanahan.
$350/500.
This weight has a very nicely detailed sulphide cast of a sitting lion. The lion rests on a colorful ground of large colored glass chippings with a lampworked tree in the background. The weight is very decorative and collectible. The all over faceting adds interest to the paperweight.

Bohemian butterfly, c. 1930. Dia. 3.25", Height 2.2". Courtesy of Gary and Marge McClanahan. $250/400.
The butterflies in the following paperweights are lampworked with small chips of glass for the decoration and pattern. Many varieties of butterflies have been found in Bohemian paperweights and quite substantial collections can be built by the dedicated collector. These four butterfly weights are a sample from the Marge McClanahan collection. Marge has collected many of the weights seen on these pages with her collection covering all styles of Bohemian paperweights.

Bohemian Butterfly. Dia. 3.2", Height 2.25". *Courtesy of Gary and Marge McClanahan.* **$250/400.**
A striking example with bright yellow wings made by using small chippings of glass that are then melted into place.

Bohemian butterfly. Dia. 3.2", Height 2.25". *Courtesy of Gary and Marge McClanahan.* **$250/400.**
Attention to detail and a steady hand were needed to create this fine example of a Bohemian butterfly. Delicate antennae emerge from the head which has white eyes.

Side view of Bohemian butterfly.
The butterfly is placed high in the glass dome over a ground of colored chippings. The weight has been faceted with cuts that reach from the base to the top of the weight.

Bohemian butterfly. Dia. 3.25". Height 2.25". *Courtesy of Gary and Marge McClanahan.* **$250/400.**
A fancy cut paperweight with four side facets and a top window to view the all white winged butterfly, with red antennae and a yellow body. The butterfly floats over a ground of glass chippings.

French Paperweights

A great many books have been written on French paperweights and the histories of the three main producers, Baccarat, Saint Louis, and Clichy, are well documented. Numerous examples of antique and modern paperweights from these companies are displayed in almost every book on the subject. I have approached this chapter with trepidation: how do I make this particular part interesting and different when so much is already known about these companies? Most of the many types of paperweights made by the three major glassworks have been photographed and recorded, with very little turning up now that is new or different. Thankfully, with the help of several large private collections, I am able to illustrate many weights which have never been photographed before or published.

Over the last ten years or so, paperweights that were previously classified as *unknowns*, i.e. weights with canes that could not be matched to either of the big three glassworks who produced paperweights in the mid-nineteenth century, are now being attributed to the Saint Mandé Glassworks. This factory was located in a village of the same name just outside Paris.

The history and production of this paperweight making concern has been researched by the French collector Phillipe Frere and by the American paperweight and cane specialist George Kulles. Mr. Kulles has written several articles for the Paperweight Collectors Association on this subject but in particular the 1999 edition has the full history of this factory with examples of paperweights and canes.

The founder of the Saint Mandé Glassworks was Joseph Nocus. Established in 1841, and although only having one tank for glassmaking, the firm did exhibit at the Paris exhibition of 1844 and won a bronze medal for its high clarity crystal and *Facon de Venice* filigree. The factory was only in existence for sixteen years and made a variety of paperweights including spaced concentrics, close packed millefiori, sulphides with garlands of canes, and scrambled and mushrooms with torsades. Fortunately for the researchers, some of these weights have been signed with a cane that says StM. When the glassworks closed down due to bankruptcy in 1857, the inventory included 15 kilograms of millefiori canes. This glassworks is now referred to as *Saint Mandé, the Fifth French Factory*.

The *Fourth French Factory* is the Cristallerie de Pantin, Pantin. Once outside the city, Pantin is now a suburb of Paris. In 1850, a glassworks was established by E. S. Monot at La Villette, near Paris and in 1859 had moved to and was incorporated in the Pantin Glassworks. In 1868, Monot was joined by Mr. F. Stumpf and the business became known as Monot and Stumpf. The company made all kinds of chemical, industrial, and decorative glass wares. In 1878, at the Universal Exposition in Paris, paperweights were displayed on their stand. A report of the exposition was sent to the US Congress by Charles Colne, assistant secretary of the US Commissioners, representing the interests of the United States. His evaluation and description of Pantin's wares are recorded as the following: "*Paperweights of solid glass, containing glass snakes, lizards, squirrels and flowers . . . air bubbles are distributed in the mass, looking like pearl drops . . . paperweights in millefiori of roses, leaves and fruit, embedded in colored glass, which had been cut in several parts before being enclosed in the glass.*"

At this late stage of the nineteenth century it would appear that Pantin was the only factory making and exhibiting paperweights at this 1878 exposition; but, it is certain that small scale production at Baccarat has continued, on and off, from the classic period through to the early part of the twentieth century. Market forces did not jus-

tify a return to large scale production until the 1950s and, of the other classic period makers, only Baccarat and Saint Louis still remains in business. Saint Louis now produces paperweights of the highest quality, thanks to a new surge of interest in collecting paperweights and a request in 1952 by the American collector and businessman, Paul Jokelson, to restart the making of paperweights with sulphide inclusions for the coronation of England's Queen Elizabeth II. It was from this point that the modern era of paperweight production was restarted by Baccarat and the Saint Louis glasshouses. This event prompted the start of the Paperweight Collector's Association Bulletin, initiated by Paul Jokelson.

The largest producer of paperweights during the nineteenth century would appear to be Clichy. The factory was named Clichy-la-Garenne and was established in 1839 in a suburb of Paris of that name by a Mr. M. Maes. It would appear that Clichy did not make weights until the late 1840s and reached a point in 1849 when they had so many orders they were struggling to meet demand. In a letter dated 1849 from Launay, Hautin and Company, who were agents for all the glass producers, to the Saint Louis Glassworks: the message was clear (*The selling of paperweights is now gone mostly (in part) to Clichy which cannot fulfill all the orders received, two furnaces are now burning with a third to be lit soon*). Clichy had become market leaders over Baccarat and Saint Louis and were now the volume producers.

Clichy sulphide with roses, c. 1850. Dia. 3". *Courtesy of Gary and Marge McClanahan. $1,500/2,000.*
This sulphide weight has all the ingredients that the public required in the mid-nineteenth century: colorful, decorative, and with a very fashionable sulphide. The weight has a garland of canes with six of the company's rose canes, which is as good as having a signature when it comes to identifying Clichy paperweights. The royal blue background frames the design beautifully.

Clichy miniature with rose cane, c. 1850. Dia. 1.75".
Courtesy of Gary and Marge McClanahan. **$1,200/1,500**.
This paperweight has a very nice combination of moss and pastry
mold canes around the edge of the weight. Moss canes were used
sparingly by Clichy and most were used in paperweights with
grounds made almost entirely of these special green canes.

Clichy miniature with green roses, c. 1850. Dia. 1.75".
Courtesy of Gary and Marge McClanahan. **$2,000/3,000**.
Equally as rare as the previous blue roses, the green versions are
made from flattened sheet glass. The sheet glass is cut and made
into a millefiori cane and drawn down to the required size. This
weight has the pink and green rose which is found in a large
proportion of Clichy weights.

Clichy paperweight with blue roses, c. 1850. Dia. 3". *Courtesy of
Gary and Marge McClanahan.* **$4,000/5,000**.
The blue Clichy rose is so rare that it is difficult to put an accurate
indication of price on it. Any paperweight with a feature such as a rose
commands an extra premium over a similar weight without a rose. A rare
blue rose is a feature that can push up the price of an ordinary paperweight
out of all proportion to a weight with an ordinary rose.

Clichy sodden snow with "C" cane, c. 1850. Dia. 3". *Courtesy of
Gary and Marge McClanahan.* **$6,000/10,000**.
A stunning variety of complex Clichy canes. Many of the canes are pressed
on the marver whilst still hot to achieve the pastry mold look. This weight
has the added attraction of a cane with a letter C in the blue cane at two
o'clock This is regarded as the most common signature cane, but very
rarely the word Clichy or parts of it can be found in special examples. The
sodden snow ground is a nice feature to highlight these very colorful canes.

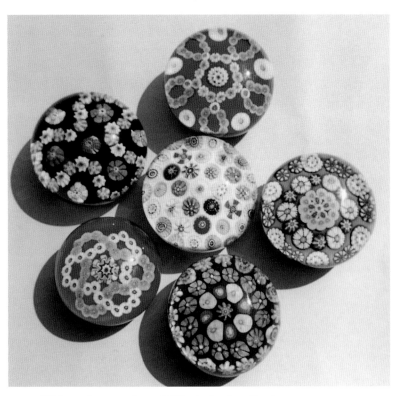

Clichy color grounds, c. 1850. *Author's collection.*
$1,500/3,000 each.
Clichy used color as a base for many designs and almost any color can be found.

Clichy scrambled with roses and signature cane, c. 1850.
Dia. 3.25", Height 2". *Author's collection.* **$5,000/6,000.**
This is a superb example of the type with two and a half large pink and green roses and elements of a purple rose; but, why you may ask is it valued at such a high price when similar pieces only sell for $2000/3000? The answer can be seen in the next photograph.

Clichy close pack with "C" cane, c. 1850. Dia. 3". *Courtesy of Gary and Marge McClanahan.* **$6,000/10,000.**
This lovely close pack is centered on a white rose with a yellow rose next to it. The rest of the canes are equally as beautiful in a wide variety of complex styles. Again the weight becomes so much more desirable when one spots the C cane in blue at the five o'clock position.

Close up of Clichy scrambled paperweight.
This close up of the same paperweight with the CLI cane also has a piece of cane that is in the shape of a dragonfly. The white insect can be seen at 9 o'clock hovering over the purple bulls-eye cane and would be a reasonable representation with respect to the minute size of this dragonfly. This has been placed deliberately in the dome of glass and cannot be a random piece of glass chipping.

52

Close up of Clichy scrambled paper-weight.

On the outer edge of this scrambled weight are the superimposed letters C L I. It would be easy to dismiss this cane as nothing more than a split cane, but the white glass supporting the green letters has been carefully folded around the letters quite deliberately. The odds against such a split cane occurring naturally must be quite phenomenal. It has been recorded that Clichy made a paperweight with an enameled letter C and a superimposed L resting on the C in a weight pictured in *Classic French Paperweights*, page 55, by Edith Mannoni, Paperweight Press, Santa Cruz, USA. On page 54 of the same book another weight can be seen with the letter C marked in the center of the weight and again in *Glass Paperweights* by James Mackay, Ward Lock, London, a paperweight by Clichy can be found on page 50 with the superimposed monogram AH. In all of these examples, the aesthetic look to the paperweight is spoiled by these large and clumsy plaques in the center of these otherwise beautiful paperweights. It would seem reasonable to assume that this superimposed CLI cane in this scrambled paperweight was an attempt by Clichy to make an identifying cane which could be reproduced easily and used in their weights. Unless, of course, it was made as a sample or after work cane by a clever worker with time on his hands and out to impress his workshop bosses. However, this is the first cane the author has ever seen of this type. Despite thorough researching of every book I could get my hands on, I have yet to find another. It may be unique . . . or is it? I would be extremely pleased to hear from anyone with a similar cane.

Close up of the base of a Clichy scrambled. *Author's collection.*

Clichy scrambled weights are probably the most interesting of all the scrambled types, including those made by Baccarat and Saint Louis, etc. You never know what lies waiting to be discovered within the jumble of whole and broken canes. Often the base of the scrambled weight can reveal many beautiful canes not available on the surface of the design and it is in this type of Clichy weight that you will have the best chance of finding an elusive C cane.

**Clichy checker paperweight with a hidden secret, c. 1850. Dia. 3",
Height 2".** *Author's collection.* **$2,500/3,500.**
The Clichy checker design is one of their best with the spaced canes
highlighted and separated by short lengths of latticinio cane. This weight has
a nice selection of brightly colored complex canes and a little secret.

**Clichy checker with white rose cane, c. 1850. Dia. 2.8", Height
2".** *Private collection.* **$1,500/2,500.**
A plain and simple checker with spaced canes and a nicely made white
and green rose cane.

Close up of Clichy checker paperweight with a hidden secret.
The secret in this paperweight is the tiny pink and green rose cane centering
this pastry mold cane. The rose cane has been drawn out to the size of a
pinhead and a strong loop is required to spot them. These tiny hidden roses
are rare, but that may be because collectors do not look for them.

**Clichy blue and white barber pole checker paperweight,
c. 1850. Dia. 3", Height 2".** *Courtesy of Gary and Marge
McClanahan.* **$5,000/7,500.**
The barber pole checker can be found in several different colors: with
red/white, and blue/white spiral cane the most common. This piece has a
lovely pink and green rose to center the paperweight with a nice
selection of large canes spaced over the surface. There is another pink
and white rose just off the edge at 1 o'clock.

**Clichy red and white barber pole checker paperweight, c. 1850.
Dia. 3", Height 2".** *Courtesy of Gary and Marge McClanahan.*
$5,000/7,500.
Centered with a white rose, this piece has a good assortment of complex
canes.

**Clichy multicolored checker paperweight, c. 1850. Dia. 3", Height
2".** *Courtesy of Gary and Marge McClanahan.* **$6,000/8,000.**
This is a very rare multicolored checker, with only one other recorded as far as
I know. The color combination gives an indication of just how many variations
in the checker weights there may be. This weight displays seven or eight
individual colored spirals which may all have been used to create this style of
checker paperweights.

Clichy pink checker paperweight, c. 1850. Dia. 3", Height 2".
Courtesy of Gary and Marge McClanahan. **$5,000/6,000.**
Very complex canes are spaced evenly over the latticinio ground with
just a little slippage in the pink spiral canes.

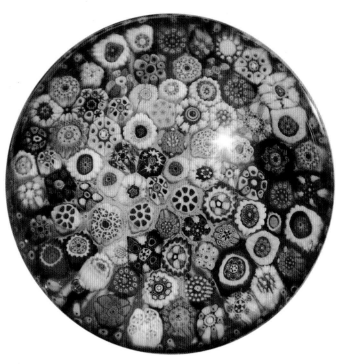

Clichy close packed paperweight, c. 1850. Dia. 2.8", Height 2.3".
Author's collection. $2,500/4,000.
A wide variety of complex canes that are to be found in Clichy weights can
be seen here. This type of paperweight was made with and without a stave
basket of canes to finish off the weight.

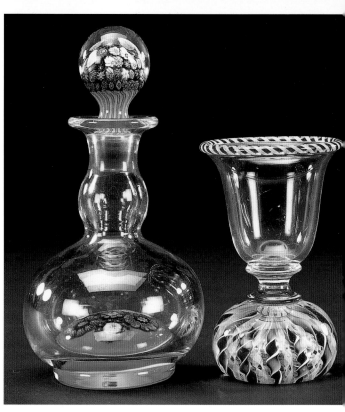

**Clichy perfume bottle, c. 1850, $8,000/12,000, and Saint Louis
spill vase, c. 1850, $4,000/6,000. *Courtesy of Sotheby's, London.***
Two magnificent examples of millefiori use, other than in paperweights.
The Clichy perfume bottle has everything you would normally find in one
of their paperweights, including a row of pink roses. The base design is set
into a turquoise blue ground with great effect. The Saint Louis spill vase
has a base made from a very desirable crown paperweight with the rim of
the piece decorated with a blue and white torsade.

Side view of Clichy close packed paperweight.
The stave basket in these blue and white collapsed canes finishes the weight off
perfectly. The basket is drawn to the center to a very neat finish.

**Saint Louis upright bouquet with torsade paperweight. Dia.
2.6", Height 1.8". *Courtesy of Gillian Murray.* $3,500/5,000.**
This is a very fine example from Saint Louis which demonstrates the
preciseness to be found in most of their paperweights. The dahlia
type flower is supported with blue and white flowers and a garland
of leaves. Nearly all upright bouquets were faceted to give the
impression that the whole dome was filled to capacity with flowers
and greenery. The torsade is another common feature of this type of
paperweight.

Saint Louis blue pelargonium paperweight, c. 1850. Dia. 2.75", Height 2". *Courtesy of Gillian Murray.* **$5,000/7,500.**

This paperweight epitomizes everything that is wonderful about Saint Louis paperweights. They were indeed a meticulous glassworks with very little leaving the factory as seconds or poorly made. This weight shouts quality with the petals made faultlessly, backed by green leaves and then set over a spiral mesh of white glass that is perfect in its construction. Saint Louis made this flower in several color combinations with red being the most common.

Saint Louis mushroom with torsade paperweight, c. 1850. Dia. 2.9", Height 2.4". *Private collection.* **$4,500/6,000.**

The mushroom weights are the same as the bouquet weights: a tight bunching of millefiori canes are drawn down to the base almost to a pinpoint in size. This example has fine combinations of complex canes neatly set and centralized within a torsade of blue and white spiral cane.

Saint Louis fruit weight, c. 1850. Dia. 2.75", Height 2". *Author's collection.* **$1,200/1,800.**

The fruit and vegetable weights made by this factory must have been very popular during the 1850s judging by the numbers made. The fruits can be found in many combinations, with apples, pears, and cherries the most common. The same is true with the vegetable examples, not quite so common as fruit weights, but can be found with carrots, turnips, marrow, and other common vegetables.

Saint Louis green jasper ground paperweight, c. 1850. Dia. 2.9", Height 2". *Private collection.* **$450/600.**

This is the most affordable of the weights made by Saint Louis and can be found in many color combinations. The ground is made from glass chippings with a single large central cane, but a nice collection can be assembled with the many varieties of this type.

57

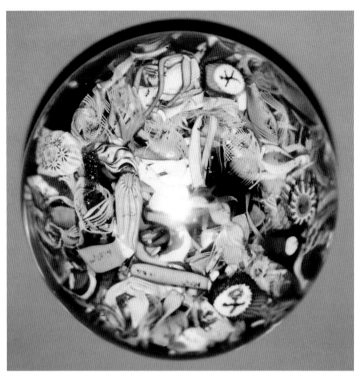

Saint Louis scrambled paperweight, c. 1850. Dia. 3.2", Height 2.5". *Private collection.* **$700/2,500.**
These end of day weights can be full of whole and broken canes, including the silhouettes seen here. The price of the weight depends very much on what is in it. The more silhouettes the higher the price. This piece has a flower and figure cane.

Saint Louis 1999 contemporary showpiece. Height 5". *Author's collection.* **$9,000/12,000.**
This is a magnificent one off example from the Saint Louis glassworks, made as a demonstration of all the wonderful artistic skills now available to the Saint Louis management, the piece is full of wild flowers and greenery made as an arrangement of buttercups, daisies, poppies, tulips, peonies, and lupins. To encase such a complex arrangement is truly masterful.

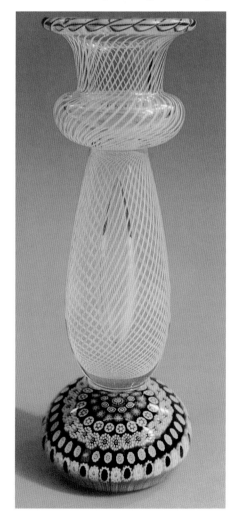

Close up of Saint Louis scrambled paperweight.
A tiny black horse is the center of this complex blue and white cane. These small silhouettes are very often overlooked and a good magnifying glass is required to spot them all.

Right:
Modern Saint Louis candlestick. Height 5.5". *Author's collection.*
$750/1,200.
Continuing with their antique heritage, the craftsmen of Saint Louis are now attaining skills that were once thought to be lost forever. The paperweight department at the factory in the Alsace region of France is only a small part of a large concern, with only six or seven workers employed full time but their output is sheer quality, with every piece aimed at the collecting market.

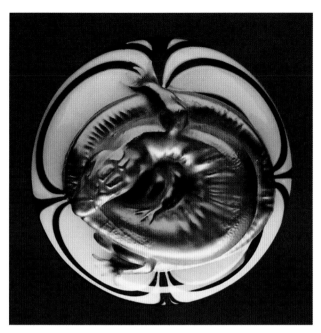

Saint Louis 1994 Salamander paperweight. Dia. 3".
Courtesy of The Cristalleries de Saint Louis, Saint-Louis-lé-Bitche, Lemberg, France. **$2,000/3,000.**
The gilded Salamander sits on a blue and white marbrie paperweight. The weight was issued as a limited edition in 1994 and retailed at $1,200. Only one hundred and fifty Salamander paperweights were made.

St. Mandé mushroom with blue and white staves, c. 1850.
Dia. 2.75". *Courtesy of Karen and Paul Dunlop. Photo ©2000 Papier Presse.* **$4,000/5,000.**
St. Mandé paperweights have been recognized as such only in the last ten years or so and thanks to several that have turned up with signature canes, it has been possible to match canes in order to identify other weights that were previously classed as unknowns. The close packed canes in this example and others following can provide the key to finding and identifying others, maybe in your own collection, that did not look quite right. One thing is certain: due to the very large variety of complex canes there must have been quite a significant production of paperweights from this Paris based concern.

Saint Louis Piedouche paperweight. Height 3.2". *Courtesy of The Cristalleries de Saint Louis, Saint-Louis-lé-Bitche, Lemberg, France.* **$3,500/5,000.**
A fabulous basket of flowers with the latticinio and blue spiral cane perfectly made. Issued in 1994 in a limited edition of one hundred and fifty.

Profile of St. Mandé Mushroom with blue and white staves.
The stave basket has been recorded in pink and white as well as this blue and white. Many rose canes appear in St. Mandé paperweights and so far George Kulles has recorded five different varieties. The pink and white rose on the bottom edge would be regarded as a four sided type with compressed flat slivers of white glass for the petals.

St. Mandé close packed with eagle canes, c. 1850. Dia. 2.7". *Courtesy of Karen and Paul Dunlop. Photo ©2000 Papier Presse.* $4,000/5,000.

This paperweight has a whole medley of colorful rose canes which look similar to the Clichy version as do the green moss canes, but there the similarity ends. It would have been easy to attribute this piece to Clichy or perhaps Bohemian before the discovery of this small but very active glassworks. The weight has white and pink rose canes and several silhouette canes of an eagle on a blue and white ground.

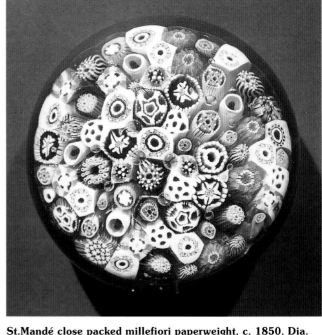

St.Mandé close packed millefiori paperweight, c. 1850. Dia. 2.8". *Courtesy of Karen and Paul Dunlop. Photo ©2000 Papier Presse.* $3,000/4,000.

Another close packed weight with a superb selection of complex canes.

St.Mandé close packed millefiori paperweight, c. 1850. Dia. 2.5". *Courtesy of Karen and Paul Dunlop. Photo ©2000 Papier Presse.* $4,000/5,000.

This very tightly packed weight has nearly two hundred very complex millefiori canes with hardly any repetition of design. Some of these canes are extremely complex themselves with sixty or seventy rods within the cane. This great diversity of color and content indicates a substantial production of paperweights but as this company was small, in comparison to Saint Louis, Clichy, and Baccarat, it would not surprise me if their output was limited to a solely French domestic market. The reasoning to this theory is that companys as small as St. Mandé do not usually export when there is a buoyant domestic demand for their product. It could be that there are hundreds of these weights waiting to be discovered in French homes and the many flea markets and antique shops that are so numerous around Northern France, and Paris in particular.

St. Mandé paperweight with spaced millefiori canes, c. 1850. Dia. 2.8". *Courtesy of Karen and Paul Dunlop. Photo ©2000 Papier Presse.* $1,500/1,800.

This paperweight has thirty-seven neatly spaced canes including several rose canes which have the petals made from collapsed tubes. Most of the canes used by this glassworks were very complex, it would be difficult to find a simply made cane in these examples.

St Mandé carpet ground paperweight of roses, c. 1850. Dia. 2.3". *Courtesy of Karen and Paul Dunlop. Photo ©2000 Papier Presse.* $2,000/3,000.
The roses in this carpet ground are made with collapsed tubes and enclosed with five green sepals made from slices of cane. The large white rose in the center is constructed from slices of white glass which enclose a very complex center. Each of the other roses are enclosed with small white stardust canes.

St. Mandé five row concentric paperweight, c. 1850. Dia. 3.2". *Courtesy of Karen and Paul Dunlop. Photo ©2000 Papier Presse.* $1,200/1,500.
This concentric is very neatly arranged over a dark ground with many of the canes made with solid rods arranged into complex canes. The canes in the center row are very unusually shaped with a pink outer layer, similar to the way a rose would be enclosed.

St. Mandé concentric paperweight on sodden snow, c. 1850. Dia. 3". *Courtesy of Karen and Paul Dunlop. Photo ©2000 Papier Presse.* $2,000/3,000.
This weight has a series of canes which have tiny pink and green roses enclosed. In total there are one hundred and four individual roses. The central red, white, and blue cane has been segmented like a grapefruit and the yellow canes around it are also full of tiny roses. This imaginative design has been set in the off white glass known as sodden snow.

St.Mandé paperweight with spokes on a yellow ground, c. 1850. Dia. 3.25". *Courtesy of Karen and Paul Dunlop. Photo ©2000 Papier Presse.* $2,000/3,000.
Six large canes have been set into an opaque yellow ground with six spokes radiating from a large hollow, white central cane. One of the spokes has been made with a row of rose canes while another arm has canes that have been described as *like a picket fence*, thin white rods lined up like a fence.

St. Mandé open concentric paperweight, c. 1850. Dia. 3".
Courtesy of Karen and Paul Dunlop. Photo ©2000 Papier Presse. **$1,200/1,500.**
Pink and white canes surround a lemon yellow central feature cane with an outer garland of nicely arranged pink and yellow canes, interspersed with solid white segments formed around a tiny red and white cog cane.

St. Mandé close pack with a frame, c. 1850. Dia. 2.9".
Courtesy of Karen and Paul Dunlop. Photo ©2000 Papier Presse. **$2,000/3,000.**
An unusual close pack with canes laid out in a square in various colors. The frame encloses a mixed variety of canes with the rest of the close packed canes tightly placed to completely fill the weight.

St. Mandé C scroll paperweight, c. 1850. Dia. 2.7".
Courtesy of Karen and Paul Dunlop. Photo ©2000 Papier Presse. **$1,500/1,800.**
A large white rose is enclosed by two rows of green and white canes which then have a series of C scrolls in red, white, and blue canes made up in a similar fashion to the Clichy and Bohemian C scrolls.

St. Mandé patterned paperweight with monogram, c. 1850. Dia. 3". *Courtesy of Karen and Paul Dunlop. Photo ©2000 Papier Presse.* **$2,500/3,500.**
The canes are set into patterns around a single cane and then the eight groups enclose a large blue plaque which has the initial L with fancy scrolls etched into the blue ground. The canes include a group of white roses with red and white complex centers.

St. Mandé close pack, c. 1850. Dia. 3.25". *Courtesy of The Vienna Art Auctions, Palais Kinsky, Vienna, Austria. $2,500/3,500.*
Another mainly blue and pink paperweight which harmonizes well. In this paperweight, several canes have blue and white and red and white arrowhead canes among a fine variety of pastel colored complex canes.

St. Mandé rose paperweight, c. 1850. Dia. 3". *Courtesy of The Vienna Art Auctions, Palais Kinsky, Vienna, Austria. $4,000/6,000.*
A lovely example of large roses with blue sepals holding the pink petals tightly furled. The six large pink roses with this unusual blue color combination surround the large white rose with dark red sepals (again an unusual color combination for a rose, but the general color combinations of blues and pinks make this a very desirable paperweight).

Base view of St. Mandé paperweight with monogram.
Tightly twisted lengths of latticinio make up the ground for the canes and plaque to rest upon.

Baccarat dated 1848 carpet ground paperweight. Dia. 3.2", Height 1.9". *Courtesy of Gary and Marge McClanahan. $8,000/10,000.*
This weight has spaced canes with silhouettes of deer, a monkey, and a swan. The silhouette canes are called Gridel canes, after Emil Gridel, the works manager at Baccarat in the mid- nineteenth century, whose young nephew had drawn the animals. Emil commissioned the canes to be made and inserted into paperweights. The carpet grounds are among the rarest of Baccarat's paperweights and can be found in several other colors.

Baccarat dated 1848 spaced on latticinio paperweight. Dia. 3.35". *Courtesy of a private collector.* $3,000/4,000.

This is a superb example of the type with six silhouettes and a flower cane to center the piece. Good strong coloring ensures the canes stand out against the lacy background which also has a few pieces of colored spiral cane amongst the feature canes.

Baccarat dated 1847 close pack paperweights. Dia. 2.5", Height 1.7". *Author's collection.* $3,000/4,000.

Close packs are the most interesting of paperweights, nearly every time you pick up a favorite piece you find another cane you had not noticed before; the interest can last for years. This weight has a tremendous variety of canes, including silhouettes, flowers, honeycombs, shamrocks and birds, and many fine and varied complex canes.

Baccarat paperweight with butterflies, c. 1850. Dia. 3" *Courtesy of Gary and Marge McClanahan.* $6,000/8,000.

This weight has a complete row of fourteen small butterflies as a garland around this special weight. The clover leaf cane is quite rare and usually found in close packed weights from this maker. The design is set over white lace, spiral canes to show off these special millefiori canes to their best effect.

Baccarat double overlay mushroom paperweight, c. 1850. Dia. 3.25". *Courtesy of a private collector.* $3,500/4,500.

Baccarat, Clichy, and Saint Louis all made this type of overlay with a mushroom bouquet. The overlay of glass can be found in several other colors including red, green, white, and a very rare yellow.

Baccarat green snake over lace paperweight, c. 1850. Dia. 3".
Courtesy of a private collector. **$8,000/10,000.**
Baccarat made several different colored snake weights, some were made on a lace ground but others were set on a rock ground. These creatures are very desirable to collectors and are very realistic in construction.

Baccarat dahlia paperweight with a garland, c. 1850. Dia. 3.2".
Courtesy of Gary and Marge McClanahan. **$3,000/4,000.**
A fine white pompom dahlia with a bud and dark green leaves framing the design. The pure white petals are gathered round the delicately made yellow stamens to create a realistic representation of this lovely autumn flower. The garland of green and white complex canes completes the picture.

Baccarat butterfly paperweight, c. 1850. Dia. 3.25". *Courtesy of Gary and Marge McClanahan.* **$4,500/6,000.**
Unlike the snake weights from Baccarat, the butterfly weights always appear a little on the coarse side. Although the wings are well made and colorful, the body seems out of proportion but the creature is fairly rare and with a garland over lace, very desirable.

Baccarat newel post, c. 1850. Height 6".
Courtesy of Sotheby's, London. **$10,000 plus.**
This show piece from Baccarat has hundreds of complex and silhouette canes, practically every cane ever used must have gone into this spectacular piece.

65

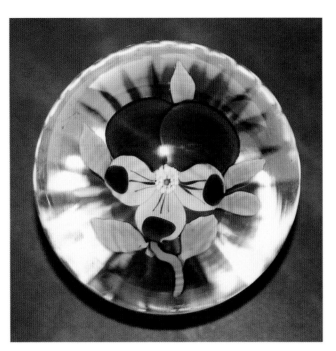

Baccarat pansy paperweight, c. 1850. Dia. 2.75". *Courtesy of a private collector.* $800/1,500.

The Baccarat factory made many varieties of flowers, but the most numerous are the pansies. These can be found with or without a garland in all sizes from a miniature at 1.75" to full size of 3.25". Most are star cut to the base and a variance in the petals and coloring is not unusual.

Baccarat pansy paperweight, dated 1889, with H R monogram. Dia. 2.75, Height 2". *Courtesy of Gary and Marge McClanahan.* $800/1,500.

Baccarat has continued to produce the popular pansy paperweight throughout the nineteenth and twentieth centuries. Dated examples of simple pansy weights have not been recorded during the classic period of 1845 to 1855; however, as this was a paperweight, probably sold at the gift shop at the very top of the Eiffel tower to commemorate the opening of this monument in Paris in 1889, it would seem appropriate that gifts were inscribed to mark this notable date which was also the centenary anniversary of the French Revolution.

Baccarat, dated 1903, pansy paperweight with M S monogram. Dia. 2.9", Height 2.3". *Author's collection.* $800/1,500.

Baccarat paperweights with amber colored lower petals are normally regarded as having been made by Mr. Dupont, a Baccarat worker of the 1920s, in an attempt to recreate some of the classic designs and styles of the 1850s. In this and the previous weight, the lower petals are of a slightly deeper coloring with inscribed dates from 1889 and 1903 respectively. The design of the pansy weights has not changed much at all from classic times to the later attributed weights. This pansy has fancy scrolling with the initials M S and the date 1903 on the sides. I would regard this paperweight as just another occasional Baccarat production piece and too early to have been made by Dupont. This weight does not conform to the size and shape normally attributed to his paperweights, which are low domed and with almost flat bases.

Side view of Baccarat, dated 1903, pansy paperweight with M S monogram.

This side view shows a very high profile, unlike the Dupont version which is usually very low.

Baccarat, dated 1854, pansy paperweight. Dia. 2.5", Height 1.5".
***Author's collection.* $500/650.**

This paperweight is generally described as *a Dupont* in honor of a Mr. Dupont, who supposedly was the only worker at Baccarat in the 1920s who knew the secrets of paperweight making. It is recorded that his weights were sold through the Baccarat retail shop next door to the Hotel Montalembert in Paris in the 1930s. Until he died in 1934, Mr. Dupont worked in great secrecy during production periods and refused to receive visitors whilst working. Dates found within the Dupont weights are spurious, with such unrealistic dates as 1815, which was thirty odd years before paperweights were thought of. There is quite a significant difference in the Dupont weights to the weights made around 1850. The base is very wide and usually flat ground or with a very shallow concavity and the dome has a very low profile. The millefiori canes are also pale in color and tend to bleed into the surrounding glass, but his lampwork pansy is almost as good as the antique versions and very collectible.

**Baccarat, c. 1930, Dupont garland paperweight. Dia. 2.75",
Height 1.6".** ***Author's collection.* $400/500.**

The Dupont garland has canes that are much smaller than the antique weight and have canes that look *washed out* and tend to bleed into the glass when looked at over a light source.

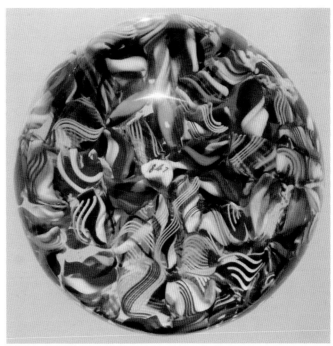

**Baccarat Dupont scrambled dated 1847 paperweight. Dia. 2.75",
Height 1.6".** ***Author's collection.* $350/500.**

A false date sits in the center of this nice Dupont scrambled weight. Although nicely made, the weight lacks the stronger colors found in antique weights.

Left:
**Baccarat, c. 1850, garland paperweight. Dia. 3".
Height 2".** ***Author's collection.* $750/900.**

Compare this strongly colored antique weight to the similar Dupont version and the differences become obvious.

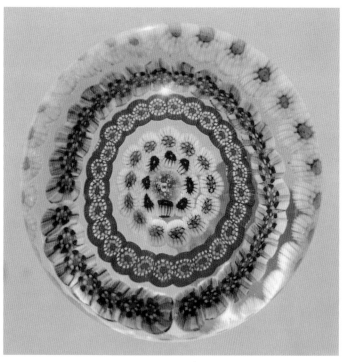

Baccarat Dupont with butterfly cane, c. 1930. Dia. 3", Height 1.7". *Author's collection.* $400/500.
Dupont paperweights also lack the precision associated with the antique types: this is slightly off center and with a slight ovality to the rings of canes. The central cane, however, is quite complex with a tiny butterfly as a center.

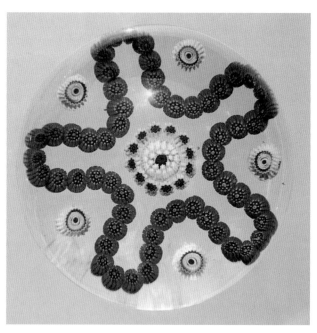

Baccarat Dupont cinquefoil paperweight, c. 1930. Dia. 2.75", Height 1.5", *Author's collection.* $350/450.
This is quite a rare design for a Dupont weight. It has a very shallow dome and flat base to identify it as Dupont.

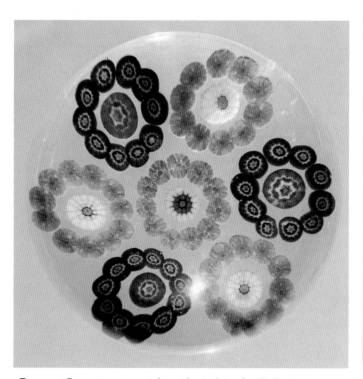

Baccarat Dupont paperweight with circlets of millefiori canes, c. 1930. Dia. 2.75", Height 1.7". *Author's collection.* $400/600.
This Dupont weight, with circlets of canes, is the most frequently found design and very often confused with the antique version.

Baccarat, c. 1980, lampworked roses and ladybug paperweight. Dia. 3.35", Height 2.25". *Author's collection.* $500/750.
This paperweight demonstrates all the skills learned in this renaissance in paperweights, by the Baccarat craftsmen. The weight has all the precise lampwork and strong colors now associated with the modern makers. From the early 1950s, Baccarat has made paperweights which are collected worldwide and as works of art are sure to appreciate in value.

Pantin Gila monster paperweight, c. 1875. Dia. 3.9".
Courtesy of Karen and Paul Dunlop. Photo ©2000
Papier Presse. **$60,000/140,000.**

The pinnacle achieved by the nineteenth century lampworkers of Pantin is clearly displayed in the three Salamanders and Gila monsters shown here. It is not just the artistry of the lampworker who created the Salamander that leaves one with a feeling of awe, but the technical ability which took place over a hundred years ago; to encase such a wonderful design is amazing. The reptile in this example of magnum proportions is foraging in the undergrowth of flowers and leaves and is one of only twelve known examples. This example has yellow spots down both flanks.

**Pantin Salamander paperweight, c. 1875. Dia. 4.25",
Height 3.25".** *Courtesy of The Vienna Art Auctions, Palais Kinsky, Vienna, Austria.* **$60,000/140,000.**

The flowers and shrubbery over a green ground would make this a desirable, magnum paperweight even without the Salamander. The reptile, made in black glass with orange spots on the head and flanks, is lying between the two tall flowers of red and white with yellow stamens. The green leaves are made by overlaying white glass with a dark green outer covering; this gives the leaves a subtle shading of light and dark green.

Pantin Salamander paperweight, c. 1875. Dia. 4.3". *Courtesy of L.H. Selman Ltd. Santa Cruz, California, USA. $140,000.*
This is one of the finest examples of its type with a very intricate lattice work of lighter colored threads infused onto the body which is colored a very dark green. The Salamander has turned its head and body, alert to its environment. The stunning flower with red inner and white outer petals is set within six ribbed leaves with a gold edging. The green moss and rocky ground give the piece a very realistic natural setting.

Left:
Pantin white flower paperweight, c. 1875. Dia. 3". *Courtesy of Karen and Paul Dunlop. Photo ©2000 Papier Presse. $20,000/24,000.*
The white petals in this flower are so delicately made as to be almost translucent. A three dimensional quality is given to the petals, which are slightly cupped and curved and are then set in four layers around a prominent set of buttercup yellow stamens. The flower, which is part of a set of serrated and contoured leaves, is so well made it looks real. Pantin paperweights usually show a multitude of tiny bubbles in the glass like boiling syrup, but in some weights it is only a minor flaw.

Pantin rose paperweight, c. 1875. Dia. 2.9". *Courtesy of Karen and Paul Dunlop. Photo ©2000 Papier Presse.* $12,000/15,000.
A rose and bud in a shade of pink which is overlaid over white glass to give the color shading to the petals. The rose head is beautifully constructed around the yellow center, but the leaves appear to have bled into the surrounding glass and spoiled the effect. This appears to have been a problem for Pantin as many of their weights, which have red and green colorings, are affected. Although Pantin weights are extremely rare, the encasing glass in many examples does not match the delicate skills of the lampworker.

Pantin white camellia paperweight over a red ground, c. 1875. Dia. 2.75". *Courtesy of Karen and Paul Dunlop. Photo ©2000 Papier Presse.* $20,000/22,000.
The rarity and artistry demonstrated in Pantin paperweights makes them the most desirable of paperweights. This superb camellia with leaves and stem, set over a tomato red ground, puts it at the top of most collectors wanted list.

Pantin fuschia paperweight over a white ground, c. 1875. Dia. 3". *Courtesy of Karen and Paul Dunlop. Photo ©2000 Papier Presse.* $12,000/15,000.
This is a lovely example of a fuschia with a fully open flower and three buds in various stages of opening. Tiny bubbles like dew drops coat the leaves, and in this volume they do not detract from the very beautiful design.

Pantin cherries paperweight, c. 1875. Dia. 2.75". *Courtesy of Karen and Paul Dunlop. Photo ©2000 Papier Presse.* $8,000/10,000.
A realistic two cherry arrangement is attached to a woody stem with serrated leaves, and then set over a clear glass ground.

Pantin grapes paperweight on a white ground, c. 1875. Dia. 2.9". *Courtesy of Karen and Paul Dunlop. Photo ©2000 Papier Presse.* $12,000/15,000.
This setting of purple colored grapes, hanging from a twisted vine with four wide leaves, is set over a white ground to frame this lovely arrangement. Unfortunately, as with many valuable items of antiquity, if it is possible to fake it then there is a good chance someone will. The following paperweights are good examples of fakes of expensive Baccarat antique wheatflowers and can easily catch out the unwary.

Pantin pink cherries paperweight set over a white ground, c. 1875. Dia. 3". *Courtesy of Karen and Paul Dunlop. Photo ©2000 Papier Presse.* $10,000/12,000.
Air bubbles like tiny pearls coat the pink cherries and leaves in this very rare and desirable arrangement.

Pantin apple paperweight, c. 1875. Dia. 3". *Courtesy of Karen and Paul Dunlop. Photo ©2000 Papier Presse.* $16,000/18,000.
A very rare and superbly made russet colored apple is backed by leaves and a stalk in this fruit offering from the Pantin glassworks.

Fake Baccarat pink wheatflower, unknown maker. Dia. 3", Height 2". *Author's collection.*
This is the first of the many fakes that are sure to follow this nicely made pink wheatflower. It was offered for auction in Scotland along with a three other weights that were catalogued as nineteenth century French. Having received a rather poor computer image of the weights, I bought these examples for a price that raised the question why so cheap? The weights were described by the auctioneer as having a shallow concavity with wear to the basal rim and one was star cut to the base. With the bidding only reaching $250 on each lot, I either had the bargain of the year or a *pig in a poke*. If it sounds too good to be true then it usually is and so it turned out. Once to hand, I realized they were indeed fakes to fool and dupe the unwary and trusting. It would have been relatively easy to prove they were not as described in the catalogue, i.e.nineteenth century French weights and receive a refund from the auctioneers, but I have a collection of fake weights so decided to keep them.

**Fake Baccarat blue wheatflower. Dia. 3.25",
Height 2.25".** *Author's collection.*
The heavy glass has been analyzed as 24% lead crystal
and has an almost white appearance. The makers of
these pieces are obviously well practiced in lampworking
and copying other peoples products but do not have the
confidence to sign their own work. However, they must
have access to a workshop. The weights do not appear to
be Chinese, although Chinese manufacturers are now
offering nineteenth century French style copies to
importers; but, the quality can be atrociously poor.

Below:
Base of blue wheatflower.
The new scratches can be clearly seen on the basal rim. The weight has
probably been rubbed over a sand covered, flat steel plate or coarse
sand paper. This method to *antique* paperweight bases was practiced
by English paperweight makers Arculus and Walsh-Walsh in the 1920s.

Base of pink wheatflower.
The base is star cut with a shallow concavity and with the
basal ring deliberately aged with new scratches. Under a
strong loop, the scratches can be seen clearly and do not
have any trace of dirt or grime from 150 years of use.

English Paperweights

English glass makers were late starters to paperweights with millefiori inclusions and although Apsley Pellat and several others had begun making sulphide medallions from the early part of the nineteenth century, these were made of a powdered glass paste and then enclosed within the body of glass. It was not until the English manufacturers began to notice the abundance of imported millefiori paperweights in stationary shops that they began to produce paperweights of a similar nature. The Bohemian and French factories had several years start on the most notable of the English makers, George Bacchus Ltd. and Islington Glassworks, who both only made millefiori weights. Lampworked weights were never produced by the English makers; by the time the necessary skills had been developed by English glassworkers, the market for these beautiful objects had seriously declined to the point where it was no longer profitable to develop the line any further. English weights from around 1850 do include many fine millefiori canes that could even be considered to surpass the French and other foreign millefiori imports in design and complexity. These weights were not just copies of foreign weights, but had a style of their own.

The Bacchus canes in particular were much larger and paler in color than their French counterparts. The closest the English makers got to anything other than concentric, close packed or spaced cane paperweights, was the inclusion of a molded silhouette of Queen Victoria which can be found in Bacchus weights in a variety of sizes, colors, and shapes. The Islington Glassworks have a black horse silhouette cane; but, apart from these very rare silhouettes, no other paperweights with anything even resembling lampwork has turned up. It would seem that not even end of the day or friggers were made with lampwork. This reluctance to produce even simple lampworked pieces has continued right up to the present day with no current maker producing flowers or lampwork of any description.

The most significant English glasshouse to produce paperweights from the earliest of times until 1980, when the company ceased trading, was the firm of Whitefriars Glass Ltd. of London. Although the company had been established for over two hundred years, no classic period (1845-1852) paperweights have ever been attributed with 100% certainty to Whitefriars. There are many *English style* paperweights that could have been made by Whitefriars or by one of the many small glasshouses that proliferated in the Birmingham and Stourbridge area during the 1850s. From the 1950s to the final days of the company's existence, Whitefriars did produce floral and other motifs that do resemble lampwork. The techniques used were unique to the company at that time: by drawing out millefiori rods to the thickness of a needle and then bundling the rods together, they were able to create forms and pictures of objects, silhouettes, and birds within the body of the cane. This technique makes these pieces, some of the most sought after and desirable of all modern paperweights.

The use of a mold to create animal shapes was also employed by Walsh-Walsh Ltd. and the Arculus Glassworks during the first half of the twentieth century.

Bacchus close packed paperweight, c. 1850. Dia. 3.5", Height 2.5". *Courtesy of Gillian Murray.* $10,000/12,000.
A magnificent close packed paperweight from the George Bacchus glassworks. This paperweight has a superb selection of canes, ranging from the very simple to extraordinarily complex. The placement of the canes around the central large red and white feature cane is beautifully executed with very little distortion to the millefiori canes. The colors are subtle shades of red, blues, mint green, and canary yellows, with whites and brown mixed in for good measure. Canes with eight cogs can be found in almost all Bacchus weights and in many other English style paperweights, with the central cane in this weight a good example of the type.

**Bacchus close packed millefiori paperweight, c. 1850. Dia. 3.6",
Height 2.25".** *Author's collection.* **$12,000/15,000.**
This close pack has a variety of canes which are unsurpassed by any of the past
or present makers. If only our contemporary millefiori cane makers could get
their canes to look like these, then I am sure collectors would be beating a path
to their door, check book in hand. It is also the soft pastel colors that add to this
beautiful paperweight. Creativity by the designers can be seen in the oak leaf
shapes in a single cane or as part of a more complex cane. Most of the canes in
this weight are of a different variety to the other close packs illustrated here.

**Bacchus close packed paperweight, c. 1850. Dia. 3.5", Height
2.3".** *Courtesy of Gillian Murray.* **$8,000/10,000.**
There are not so many varieties of canes in this example, but the
complexity of several are quite staggering. The mint green and pink
cane at four o clock is particularly nice as the color combination is
perfectly matched. The mint green canes are seen as single elements
and also as a complex cane. The outer row of blue and white canes are
drawn to the center of the base, to create a basket, and then finished off
neatly with a small porthole window.

**Close up of Bacchus close
packed millefiori paper-
weight.**
The oak leaf cane can be clearly
seen toward the bottom of the
photograph as a single element,
but to the top right of the
photograph, the oak leaf is also
the center of a very complex cane.

Bacchus five row concentric, c. 1850. Dia. 3.5", Height 2.3". *Courtesy of Gillian Murray.* **$10,000/12,000.**
The central yellow cane in this weight is particularly nice because it looks as though it has been crafted around the central red and white millefiori part. This was done by drawing the enclosing yellow, flared tube down to a small tapered funnel, to hold the cane in place, almost like a *bouquet de marriage*. The other canes are simply made tubes and stars which are then encased with a white collar. The dark blue coloring also enhances the beautiful arrangement in this very desirable Bacchus weight. An unseen outer row of blue and white cog canes are drawn down to the center of the base.

Bacchus four row concentric, c. 1850. Dia. 3.4", Height 2.4". *Courtesy of Gillian Murray.* **$8,000/10,000.**
The central feature cane is again very beautiful in its construction and design and worthy of its central position. At times Bacchus weights can be a little slipshod in cane placement, but in this very fine example the canes are meticulously placed with no slippage. The very complex pink and blue canes have been called Greek shield canes by George Kulles (author of *Identifying Antique Paperweights*, Paperweight Press, Locust Street, California, USA), as the cane resembles the round, decorated shield carried by ancient Greek warriors into battle.

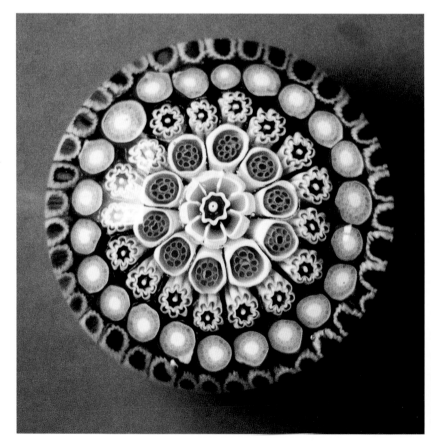

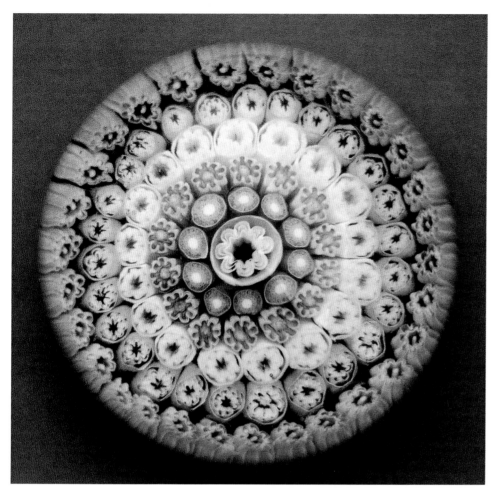

Bacchus five row concentric, c. 1850. Dia. 3.5", Height 2.5". *Courtesy of Gillian Murray.* **$10,000/12,000.**
Another special central cane with a row of Greek shield canes encircling it. The central row of canes are formed from over forty small complex canes grouped together to make an even more complex cane which also has a stardust millefiori center. In the nineteenth century, the production of canes of this complexity was, and still is, very labor intensive. This would have made this item very expensive to produce. Unfortunately, we have no idea what a Bacchus weight would have been sold for at retail price but it was far beyond the means of the working classes. Because so few paperweights were made by Bacchus, it is possible production was stopped because of the very complexity and manufacturing cost of their canes. It has been estimated that only four hundred weights were made by Bacchus, c. 1850, and because they are so beautiful, it is possible that the great majority have survived to the present day, albeit sometimes with a few bruises and scratches. Most Bacchus weights are now known and have been photographed at some stage of their existence, but occasionally a new weight does turn up that is unknown to the specialist paperweight collectors.

Bacchus seven row concentric, c. 1850. Dia. 3.5", Height 2.5". *Courtesy of Gillian Murray.* **$12,000/15,000.**
Paperweights of this quality are few and far between, even from the Bacchus glassworkers. The seven rows are set out precisely around an eight cog central feature cane and could almost qualify as a two color carpet ground weight. Another row of the darker canes is just out of sight below the outer edge which is pulled down and under to the base center. The canes are complex with the central feature cane being perfectly repeated in miniature in two of the darker red rows.

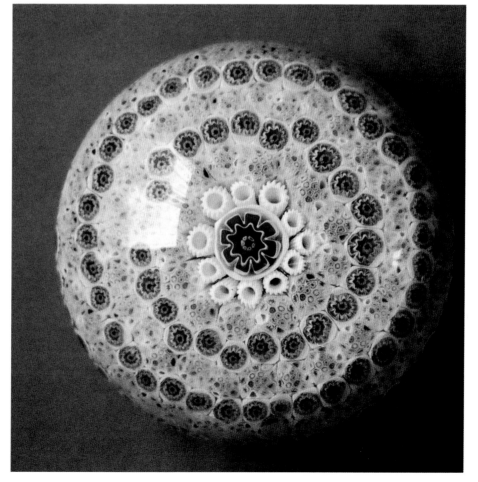

Bacchus close packed paperweight, c. 1850. Dia. 2.75", Height 1.9". *Author's collection.* **$3,000/4,000.**

This close pack is a recent purchase from an antique fair in the UK and was previously in the possession of a Birmingham family who have had the weight passed down as far back as anyone in the family could remember. Although on the small side for a Bacchus weight, which tend to be 3.5 inches, the weight had not been reground until I had several shallow scratches removed which made very little difference to its original size and shows that occasionally a new weight will turn up that is an unknown Bacchus; however, this is a very rare occurrence.

Bacchus concentric with silhouette and spaced canes, c. 1850. Dia. 3.5", Height 2.5". *Author's collection.* **$1,000/1,500.**

A lovely full size Bacchus paperweight at a bargain price? With a nicely centered silhouette, there is also plenty of variety in the tubes and complex canes, so why is it priced so reasonably when Bacchus prices are spiraling ever higher? Unfortunately this weight has several very large annealing cracks radiating away from the unground pontil mark. Fortunately, the cracks cannot be seen from above and it is displayed with pride. It is very rare to come across a Bacchus weight with annealing cracks and this is only the second this author has seen. In perfect condition, I would expect a piece such as this to fetch $4000/5000 or more at auction.

Bacchus six row concentric with silhouette, c. 1850. Dia. 2.75", Height 1.8". *Courtesy of Annemarie and Gerd Mattes.* **$3,000/4,000.**

This Bacchus paperweight has a silhouette of a young Queen Victoria in dark glass on a white ground with six rows of slightly uneven open tubes and eight cog canes. One of the outer rows has as many as forty small elements making a complex cane. One row cannot be seen from above and although slightly off center, the weight is still on the desirable list for most collectors.

Base of six row Bacchus with silhouette.

The base shows the precise finish achieved by the Bacchus glassworkers. The outer row of tube canes has been drawn to the center where the pontil was snapped off and ground out to a slight concavity, leaving a small window to view the interior. All six rows can be viewed through this window.

Bacchus inkwell, c. 1850. Dia. 2.9", Height 4.5". *Courtesy of Annemarie and Gerd Mattes.*
This is a very rare and elegant inkwell with a pewter top, which has probably been a later addition to the piece. The sides are faceted with six elongated cuts from the base to the top of the neck. There is a lid for this piece which has a damaged hinge and it is topped with a finial. The canes are of the Bacchus type with eighteen cog canes, which have only been found in Bacchus pieces so far, and the piece is centered by a Queen Victoria silhouette cane. The whole piece sits on a crystal foot.

Islington Glassworks paperweight, c. 1850. Dia. 2.7", Height 1.8". *Private collection.*
A superb example of this very rare type of paperweight showing black horse silhouettes among a varied selection of colorful canes. With this many varieties of millefiori canes, there must surely be quite a few more than have been seen in the four examples from this glassworks that have been recorded to date. It would not be unreasonable to assume that 50 or a 100 more exist somewhere out there, just waiting to be recognized for what they are.

Bacchus inkwell with stopper, c. 1850. Height approx. 5". *Courtesy of a private collector.*
It is difficult to assess the value of any object when only two or three pieces are known to exist and these pieces have never sold at auction. Therefore, prices given for an inkwell could be wildly wrong in both cases. This piece shows the elegant tapering of the neck to a flared rim and a matching stopper in place. The canes are typically Bacchus in style and coloring, with the workmanship outstanding in cane quality and in the construction of the whole piece.

Islington mantle ornament . Dia 2.75", Height 4.75". *Courtesy of Terry and Hilary Johnson.* **$2,500/3,500.**
The usual description for this type of object would be wig or mantle ornament but it fits very nicely in the hand and may have been designed as a paperweight to hold down paper on someone's desk. As a wig stand it would seem to be too low. The canes in this piece are exceptionally complex with the white star dust canes comprising some 100 segments to make up a single cane. The blue and white row of canes in this piece match canes found in Islington weights which are illustrated in Identifying Antique Paperweights Millefiori, by George Kulles. The pink inner row of canes are formed as a honeycomb. The piece is faceted all over with a very elaborate cutting to the base.

Close up of the top of the Islington mantle ornament.
The canes in this piece are extraordinarily complex, as can be seen in the white row around the central feature cane. This cane is in sixteen oblong sections, translucent in places and lacy thin. The whole object has the "English" look and feel to it with soft pastel coloring and fluoresces exactly the same as Bacchus weights.

Islington mantle ornament. Dia. 3", Height 4.75". *Author's collection.* **$2,500/3,500.**
This piece is very similar to the previous weight. The white star dust canes are identical and a very complex and rare honeycomb cane formed with square tubes can be seen around the centre of the weight. This tube cane is very similar to the known Islington examples in its make up.

Bacchus all white carpet grounds, c. 1850. *Private collection.*
Even when Bacchus made weights with little or no color, the results are quite spectacular. My photography does not do justice to the exquisite nature of these very special white grounds. The outer row of colored canes are pulled beneath the weight to form a basket to hold the white millefiori.

Bacchus display case at PCA convention, Chicago 1999.
The Chicago convention was a memorable event for Bacchus lovers, as over 100 Bacchus weights were on display in the largest gathering of examples from this English manufacturer ever seen in one place. Many of the paperweights on display had never been exhibited before. The opportunity to see the enormous variety of weights by Bacchus has helped with the identification of some unknowns.

Bacchus concentric with seven Queen Victoria silhouette canes, c. 1850. *Private collection.*
The white, eight cog ruffle canes are from the same mold that formed the elements that go into most Bacchus paperweights. The millefiori and silhouette canes selected are placed on a clear ground set around a central, very complex cane.

Bacchus concentric with cross canes, c. 1850.
Courtesy of Bill Volkman. **$3000/4000.**
This paperweight has a white cross set in a red casing of glass within a tube, which is then set in an 18 cog sleeve. This should help to attribute many paperweights that are usually classed as *English, unknown maker.*

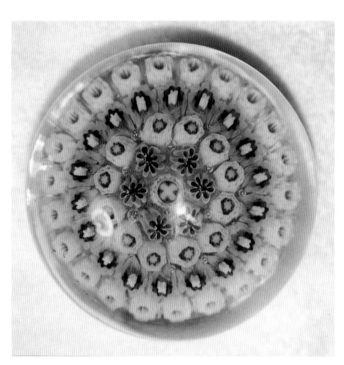

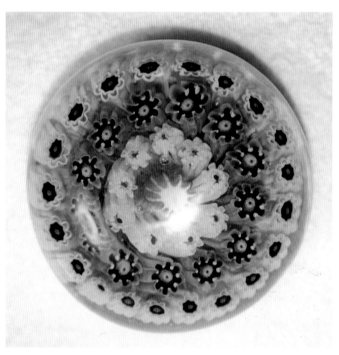

Later Bacchus paperweight with central cross, c. 1870.
Private collection.
The central cross cane is identical to that in the previous example. The same eight cog mold is used in this weight to form most of the canes. Perhaps Bacchus had a variety of eight cog molds that could be used to create slight variations to the edges of the canes . . . or is this just a variation created by the glassmaker in his handling of the hot metal?

Later Bacchus concentric paperweight, c. 1870.
Private collection.
A simple, softly colored weight, with every element of the millefiori canes made using an eight cog mold. The central feature is a solid red and white twelve cog cane. The dark blue canes are encased in an almost translucent covering of white glass. The thinness of the white covering glass has been found in many Bacchus weights; it softens and gives a lacy look to any deep color it encases.

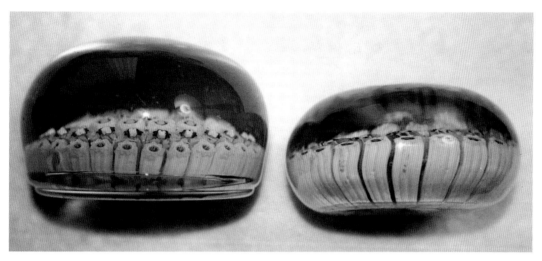

Side view of later Bacchus concentric paperweights.
The side view shows a very significant difference in the techniques used to create them. The weight on the left shows a typical Bacchus size, 3.5" x 2.5", but with short cut lengths of cane. Whilst that on the right looks as though it is from another maker, featuring long cane lengths drawn beneath the weight and a very low profile. These differences can only be explained by assuming they were made during the very early days of Bacchus paperweight production, during the experimental and learning times, or that they were made during a renaissance in paperweight making 20 or 30 years after the classic period (1845 to 1852).

Base of later Bacchus concentrics.
The only thing these weights have in common is the un-ground pontil mark. The example on the left has very short canes whereas that on the right exhibits a normal Bacchus feature: The canes are drawn into the center to a small porthole. Although this cane arrangement is slightly off center, the stave finish is good and was either adopted as the norm for further production or was an attempt to recreate the artistry shown in the beautifully precise Bacchus bases of classic period weights.

**Later Bacchus paperweight with cross cane, c. 1870. Dia. 3.3",
Height 2.5".** *Private collection.* **$2,000/3,000.**
This close packed weight has everything needed to qualify it as a Bacchus
weight: cross canes, Victoria heads, eighteen cog and eight cog canes, cruciform
rods, canes with encasing tube, and the soft pastel shades associated with
Bacchus.

Later Bacchus with tube and cross cane, c. 1870. *Private
collection.* **$1,000/1,500.**
The central spiraling cane has a white tube encasing it. This is another
Bacchus feature.

**Close up of Bacchus
paperweight with
cross cane.**
The all-white cruciform cane
can be clearly seen
alongside another white
cane that also appears in
other Bacchus weights. This
eight cog cane has a small
point on the end of each
cog and is fairly common in
weights of this type and era.

English millefiori and Queen Victoria sulphide paperweight, c. 1850. Dia. 2.8", Height 1.7". *Courtesy of Terry and Hilary Johnson.* **$600/800.**

This is a very distinctive sulphide of Queen Victoria set over three rows of simple millefiori canes with crosses. Identical canes can be found in another sulphide paperweight on page 13 of *Old English Paperweights*, Schiffer Publishing, Atglen, PA, USA, by this author. The canes are of a type that are unknown to me and others whom I have asked for an opinion. It is probable that this is from another unknown maker trading in the Birmingham area of England in the mid-nineteenth century, who shall remain anonymous for the time being.

Later Bacchus Inkwell, c. 1870. Dia. 3.5", Height 6". *Author's collection.* **$2,000/2,500.**

This is a very unusual inkwell that may or may not have been made at Bacchus. In its favor are the eight cog canes with squared off ends that are a familiar sight in many Bacchus weights and the white collars enclosing some of the canes. It also fluoresces a Bacchus color. Against it is the unusual shape to the inkwell's upper body and the wide low shape of the inkwell's main body; but, remove the top part and the foot and you have a Bacchus weight. In the previous two inkwell examples from Bacchus, the body shape is totally different. The contours of many later English inkwells vary enormously, even in examples from the same glassworks.

Close up of later Bacchus inkwell.
The inkwell has a nice selection of simple and complex canes with the second row from the edge having a Bacchus type white tube encasing the complex center.

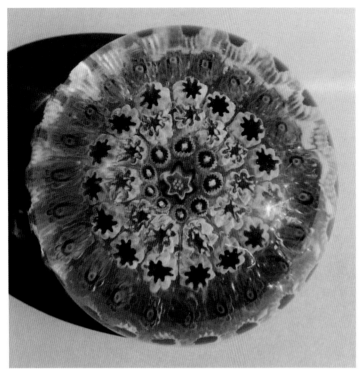

Later Bacchus concentric millefiori paperweight, c. 1870. Dia. 3.75", Height 2". *Author's collection.* **$1,200/1,500.**
This paperweight, and others similar in style, are one of the enigmas of old English paperweights. The canes appear to have been made from the same dies and molds as some classic Bacchus canes. The central blue and white canes with a small white cross are eighteen cog canes, thought to have only been used in Bacchus weights. Indeed, I have not found another in any other firm's paperweights. The larger canes with eight cogs are of a type that is very common in Bacchus weights made in the classic period. It is possible that these weights were made later, or even earlier, than the Bacchus weights we immediately recognize as classic Bacchus of the finest quality.

Base of later Bacchus concentric millefiori paperweight.
The base shows a preciseness in the setting up of the concentric rings which points to a quality maker, experienced in this procedure. The set up is picked up with a gather of glass which leaves a ridge between the canes and covering dome of glass. This trait is found in modern Whitefriars and many other old English weights.

Close up of later Bacchus concentric millefiori paperweight.
This close-up shows the eighteen cog canes around the central red and white cane with a stardust cluster. The other canes are comprised of the eight cog canes with the slightly flattened cogs. The colors are soft with the exception of the deep blue canes with eight cogs.

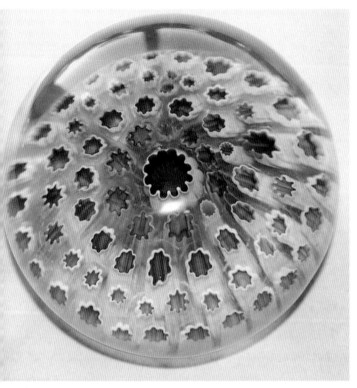

**Four row concentric paperweight later Bacchus, c. 1870. Dia. 3.5",
Height 2". *Courtesy of Annemarie and Gerd Mattes.* $450/600.**
This paperweight is of a type that is relatively common in England and it
would appear that this concentric style with these hollow tube canes were
made in considerable numbers. It is very neatly made with eight cog canes
in soft pastel shades. As a comparison to these canes, a very basic Bacchus
cane of all white construction can be seen on page 24 of *Old English
Paperweights*, Schiffer Publishing, by this author. Many of these paperweights, which almost look like a Bacchus but just miss a matching cane to
attribute precisely, can almost certainly be regarded as another Bacchus
production paperweight. Perhaps this weight is of a type that was made by
Bacchus to be sold alongside their more expensive paperweights. Many
English paperweights have a Bacchus look and feel about them that makes
me confident that this theory is almost certainly right. I have fluoresced
many of this type of paperweight and all do fluoresce exactly the same
color in long and short waves as Bacchus weights of the finest quality
usually attributed to the 1850s. Bacchus paperweights fluoresce powder
blue in the short wave and a hazy green in the longwave.

**English four row concentric within a basket, later Bacchus,
c. 1870? Dia. 3", Height 2". *Courtesy of Peter and Sandra
Williams.* $1,000/1,200.**
A first in English paperweights, as I have never come across a basket of
spiral canes encasing the rows of canes before. A large eight cog, red and
blue open cane sits in the center of the weight precisely. The spiral twists
of red, white, and blue are very well made and set neatly, almost vertical.
The other canes are based on the eight cog basic cane and have spaced
bubbles at regular intervals as further decoration to a lovely and very rare
weight.

Base of English four row concentric within a basket.
The base shows the spiral outer row drawn down to a perfect finish in the
center of the weight, but the pontil has been left unground and slightly
recessed so it would appear that the maker thought it unnecessary to
grind out the pontil. The weight rests on a thin basal ring which shows
plenty of wear. Bacchus were the masters in perfecting the technique of
drawing the outer row to the center of the base and hiding any irregularities in the cane ends.

**Engraved 1872 tankard, later Bacchus.
Height 5".** *Author's collection.* **$500/750.**
This millefiori tankard has the date 1872 heavily
engraved within a border of fern type scrolls and
tied at the bottom with a ribbon motif. The name
H. Holt is inscribed in large letters above the date.
Perhaps with further investigation it may be
possible to find out who H. Holt was and if he was
an employee of a Birmingham glasshouse in 1872.
The heavy engraving of the glass is a feature of
many Bacchus vases, etc. made around this time.

Close up of later Bacchus tankard.
Canes have been found in many old English paperweights that I have seen over the years which
are thought to be from the Birmingham/Stourbridge area of England and include the eighteen cog,
eight cog, and sometimes a ruffle cane, that leave me personally convinced that they are indeed
Bacchus paperweights. The firm of George Bacchus was taken over by Stone, Fawdrey and Stone
in 1860. Conjecture would seem to point to a renaissance in paperweight making by the new
owners, at some stage, during their occupation of this glasshouse. My reasoning is that the molds to
make the basic canes would still be on the premises as part of the inventory purchased by Stone,
Fawdrey and Stone. It may have been that paperweight production did not restart until twenty or so
years after the classic weights had ceased to be produced for whatever reason.
This would explain why these later Bacchus weights are slightly different to the earlier pieces in
terms of cane quality and restricted in design. There appears to have been very little experimentation in cane design with these later pieces, unlike the classic period
Bacchus weights which show all aspects of paperweight making within the
constraints imposed by millefiori canes only. In this earlier period, Bacchus
made weights using concentric, patterned, sodden snow, overlays,
torsades, carpet grounds, paneled, close packed, baskets, and spaced
millefiori paperweights. The later period weights show very little variation
in the use of millefiori rods, usually just concentrics or close packs. The
later weights are similar in size to early pieces in that they are usually very
large weights, around 3.5" in diameter and over 2" high, but can be
beautifully made with precise settings which would also indicate an
established glasshouse. The later Bacchus look-a-likes also fluoresce the
same colors as the classic Bacchus weights.
We have no evidence to suggest that these weights were ever made by
another glasshouse and it would seem reasonable to assume that an old
established glassworks with a history of paperweight making would
attempt a revival, such as we have seen at the major French glasshouses
over the years. Attempts to recapture the ancients artistry in cane making
has not resulted in exact copies. The results are usually not quite as good
or as varied as the originals. A parallel can be found with the modern day
production from the French glassworks of Baccarat and Saint Louis. Their
present work has a look and feel that is different to their antique equivalents, especially when antique weights are compared to the so called
Dupont weights made after c. 1920. A Mr. Dupont worked at Baccarat
and made paperweights in an attempt to recreate classic paperweights in
an antique style. As an example, if we take an antique Baccarat close pack
with its tremendous variety of complex canes and place it next to the
modern version and a Dupont close pack, the difference is obvious. The
differing styles, colors, and cane compositions shout out to you that they
were made in different eras, but they are still all Baccarat paperweights.
It is my opinion that paperweights and related objects with Bacchus type
look-a-like canes were indeed an attempt to revive the skills of the earlier
artists who had made such wonderful paperweights in the 1850s. The
trading name of George Bacchus was kept in use until c. 1890 when the
company integrated with other glasshouses and the name George
Bacchus was abandoned.

Top view of 1872 English tankard, later Bacchus.
The canes are set as a close pack and the blue and white cane near the side
is an eighteen cog cane which is thought to have been made only by
Bacchus. Several others also are eight cog and ruffle canes, some with a
white collar.

Arculus checker paperweight, c. 1920. Dia. 2.8", Height 1.8".
Author's collection. $750/1,000.
The firm of Alfred Arculus was started in 1875 and produced glassware and chandeliers until it was taken over by John Walsh-Walsh Ltd. in 1931. After a name change to the parent company, the glassworks continued to make paperweights, inkwells, and many related objects in an antique style with a spurious date inserted. This checker paperweight made in the style of a French Clichy paperweight from the classic period, c. 1850, lacks the precision achieved by the French makers and is quite a crude attempt. However, it is very rare, with only two or three others known and is a welcome addition to my collection. It could have been made at any time during the firm's existence. The clusters of millefiori canes can be matched to paperweights held by the Arculus family.

Close up of wine glass.
The close up shows a very distinctive cane around the central star cane, which is found in many of this firm's millefiori products. It is usually called a seven and six cane for want of a better description, but may have had some significance to the company as it is found so often. Could it be a signature cane?

Arculus/Walsh-Walsh wine glasses, c. 1930. Height 4". ***Courtesy of Annemarie and Gerd Mattes. $1,000/1,200 per set of six.***
The Arculus and Walsh-Walsh firms specialized in all kinds of drinking glasses and decanters, so this set is a tribute to their craftsmanship. The paperweight bases in the glasses are all set neatly and each glass has a different base. Apparently the firm did not make matched sets as far as I know. It is unusual to see a set of six as damage and loss over the years has usually reduced the set.

Close up of wine glass.
This close up shows a sitting white rabbit as the central feature cane in this glass. The rabbit is a welcome addition to any millefiori piece, adding interest and value; but, even rarer is a white horse silhouette that is known to exist as a cane. I have been unable to locate a photograph of any millefiori piece with it present. The horse is in a collection of canes held by the Broadfield House Glass Museum, King Swinford, England, and may never have been used in a paperweight.

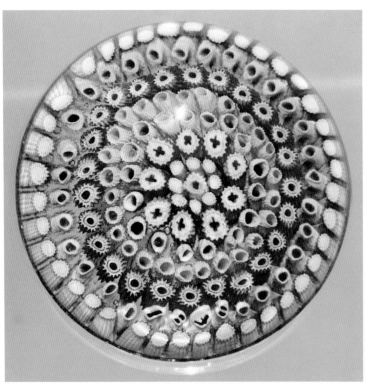

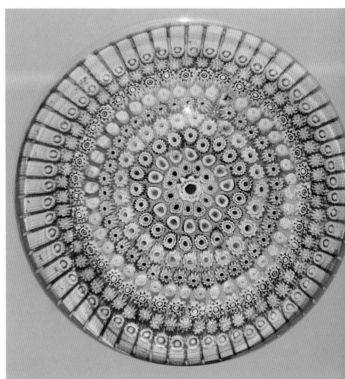

Arculus/Walsh-Walsh seven row concentric with 1848 date cane, c. 1930. Dia. 3.25", Height 1.7". *Author's collection.* **$750/1,000.**
The dated 1848 paperweights were long thought to have been made by the Whitefriars company who had traded in glass from 1834 to their closure in 1980. It is most likely that a glasshouse of their size and standing would have made paperweights at some stage in the nineteenth century, but the earliest recorded paperweights and inkwells were not catalogued until c. 1930. Millefiori canes were known to have been used by Whitefriars and can be seen in a vase held by The Museum of London, England, which can be dated to 1876. This paperweight however, was produced by the Arculus/Walsh-Walsh glassworks in Birmingham, England, in the 1920/30 period. The canes can be matched with canes held by the Broadfield House Glass Museum, who were given the canes by a man who had worked at Arculus/Walsh-Walsh in the 1930s. The company made *antiqued* pieces with false dates but only put in the 1848 date. An interesting piece of further evidence to support this comes from a conversation I have had with Colin Terris of Caithness Glass, Scotland. Colin tells me that the late Ken Wainwright, who was the manager of the Caithness Oban Studio for many years, started his glass career with Walsh-Walsh in 1937, aged just 14. He worked alongside his father and told Colin many stories of his days with the Walsh-Walsh company and often referred to making paperweights with an 1848 date cane.

Arculus/Walsh-Walsh magnum nine row concentric, c. 1930. Dia. 4", Height 1.7". *Author's collection.* **$800/1,000.**
Nine rows of simple cog canes in a variety of pinks, blue, and pale yellow make this weight special if only because it has nine rows. The canes are ordinary but nine rows is an excellent achievement by any standard. The canes must have been set in a die to achieve such preciseness, with only a little slippage to be seen. The magnum size should indicate a large dome, but with many of the paperweights made by these firms, the dome is very low in comparison. The weight shows a line of striation which slightly distorts the canes.

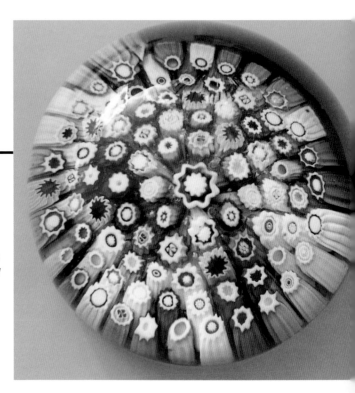

Arculus/Walsh-Walsh concentric with 7/6 canes, c. 1930. Dia. 3.4", Height 2". *Author's collection.* **$400/600.**
A close packed weight which could have been made at any time between 1915 and the early 1950s when the company ceased trading. The 7/6 canes can be seen in a variety of colors and may just be a squeezed cane, but this cane appears so frequently within their weights and inkwells, sometimes as the central featured cane, that I think it may have been either a signature cane or some kind of identifying cane. In this weight, it appears at least eight times in a variety of colors.

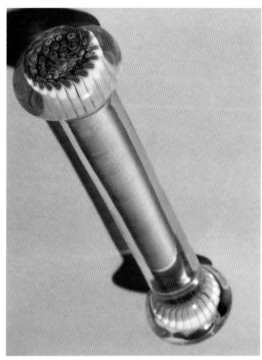

Arculus/Walsh-Walsh millefiori tankard, c. 1930. Height 5". *Courtesy of Annemarie and Gerd Mattes.* **$400/600.**
Green and white, and red and white simple cog canes make up the concentric rows in this well made tankard. The canes sit over a sturdy foot in this quite substantial tankard, which suggests it was designed to be used rather than ornamental.

Right & Above right:
Arculus/Walsh-Walsh tea cup and knife rest, c. 1930. *Courtesy of Annemarie and Gerd Mattes.* **$200/250 for tea cup, knife rest $250/400.**
The company made many different articles using millefiori canes as can be seen in these two items. Both are quite rare and the knife rest would be a welcome addition to a collection for one of the many who collect such items. The Saint Louis or Baccarat equivalent would sell for approximately $500/750 as knife rests are very collectible items.

Close up of 7/6 canes.

Walsh-Walsh, super magnum inkwell and tumbler, c. 1930. Diameter of inkwell 6", Height 8.5", $2,000/2,500. Diameter of tumbler 3.5", Height 4.5", $200/250. *Author's collection*.

This massive inkwell is the largest inkwell I have ever seen containing millefiori canes and has many canes that can be linked to the Walsh-Walsh glassworks. Unusually, the matching stopper has a finial to finish the top. It is an impractical piece to use as an inkwell and must have been a commission or exhibition piece for a trade show perhaps. The tumbler has the same canes as the inkwell; however, this tumbler was purchased separately at an auction and was formerly part of Mrs. Applethwaite Abbot's collection. The tumbler had her collection and the auction catalogue numbers and name on the base. The canes in both pieces are set as close packs and the canes are simple cogs and stars.

English inkwell by an unknown maker. Height 5". *Author's collection*. $750/1,000.

Four rows of colorful canes in the base with three rows in the stopper, of which two match those in the base: the same central feature cane is in both parts. Although I cannot match the canes to Arculus or Walsh-Walsh, it could be a piece made at this factory in the 1930/1950 period . . . or is it an antique from the nineteenth century? No other English manufacturer has come to light in this period, but a reference in the book *Paperweights* by John Bedford, published by Cassel, London, in 1968 refers to the Stourbridge firm of Davis, Greathead & Green and Thomas Hawkes and Company of nearby Dudley. Both firms are said to have "*made paperweights in the early days that were much larger than the continental variety and had a beaded foot.*" Most inkwells and early English paperweights that cannot be linked to the known Birmingham makers usually have this foot. Further research into the history of these two now defunct glassworks may lead to another English name in paperweight production.

English inkwell by unknown maker, 1917. Height 5". *Author's collection*. $1,000/1,200.

This is a quality piece by an unknown maker. The canes are set out very precisely and cannot be matched to the other Birmingham makers, Arculus and Walsh-Walsh. The inkwell has a very nice Sterling silver attachment to the stopper which may be a later addition but looks as though the glass has been molded into the holder if this is possible with the two materials coming together at different temperatures? The silver is hallmarked with the date of 1917 and the Birmingham assay office mark of a lion and anchor. The makers initials are clearly seen as CTB. Hoping that this piece would lead me to an unknown Birmingham paperweight maker, I researched the initials, only to find that they belonged to an unknown silversmith who had made the silver holder, probably as a one off commission.

English miniature inkwell by an unknown maker. Height 3". *Author's collection.* **$600/800.**
Miniature inkwells or scent bottles are very rare. The canes in this one are very ordinary with a cogged cane as a central feature which is common in English concentric millefiori pieces.

Base of Royal Brierley Crystal paperweight.
The base of this weight is in the Birch green color with the pontil removed on the grinder. The company label was stuck on each paperweight made.

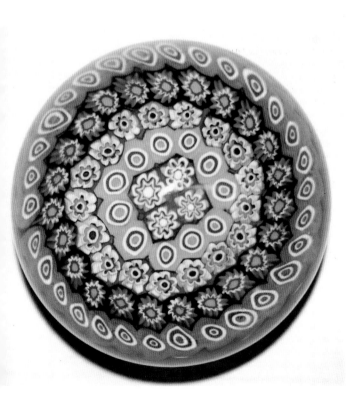

Royal Brierley Crystal 1997 concentric paperweight. Dia. 3", Height 2.2". *Courtesy of Zvi Klemer.* **$250/300.**
This paperweight is one of only fifty made by Royal Brierly Crystal Glassworks in Stourbridge, England, and as such is a very rare collectors piece. The company does not intend to make any more millefiori paperweights in the foreseeable future. The paperweights were made using Murano canes as this was more economical than making their own. I found a paperweight at an antique fair in 1999 with the Royal Brierley label on the base. On contacting the firm to find out if this was the start of a paperweight production run, the company told me that only fifty paperweights had been made and sold through their own outlet in Stourbridge. There would not be any more produced by the factory. The reasons given were that the weights proved very difficult to make and labor intensive with the resulting high cost at retail. The company spent six weeks trying to perfect the millefiori paperweight process, with a certain degree of success, and produced a trial production using four designs, on two colored bases, birch green and lapis blue. The weights were made in one size only and the four designs were identified by the most predominant cane colors: orange/green canes with green base, blue/white canes with blue base, yellow/red canes with blue base, and green/light green canes with a green base. However, the resulting problems, including bleeding in the cane, a slight incompatibility of their 24% lead crystal glass with the Murano canes, and the very high production cost decided them against a full production run. All of the paperweights were made by Wally Pinches and any remaining unused canes are still in the workshop stores.

93

Royal Brierley crystal paperweight, 1997. Dia. 3", Height 2.2".
***Author's collection.* $250/300.**
This Lapis blue based paperweight could easily be mistaken for its Italian cousins in Murano, but thankfully the company stuck a label identifying the maker on each one of the 50 made. However, I am sure that in the not too distant future a few will turn up as "Murano" paperweights due to the canes originating from there and the label being scratched away.

Whitefriars very rare white overlay paperweight, 1972. Dia. 3", Height 2.1". ***Private collection.* $1,500/2,000.**
This paperweight is an experimental piece made in 1972 with a date cane and the White Friar logo. Eventually the overlay technique was mastered, but in this piece they have used powdered glass chippings to create an overlay. The method simply was to roll the hot glass into white powdered glass and then heat at the glory hole until the glass had fused together; the process may have been repeated several times to get the depth of white glass required. The facets reveal the very rough edges to the white glass where it has not fused together. This technique was also used by Paul Ysart in his early experimentation with overlays. The Whitefriars company made very few overlay paperweights, but did eventually produce a very limited number that may only amount to single figures; but, they did make a few single flash overlays which are extremely rare.

Base of Whitefriars magnum paperweight.
The base reveals the typical cane set up and finish used by Whitefriars in all their modern production. The canes are cut to a uniform length and the pontil is removed by grinding. In this weight the pontil is left unground and indicates an early piece by Whitefriars. From 1970 onwards all paperweights were left with ground bases to remove all traces of the pontil marks.

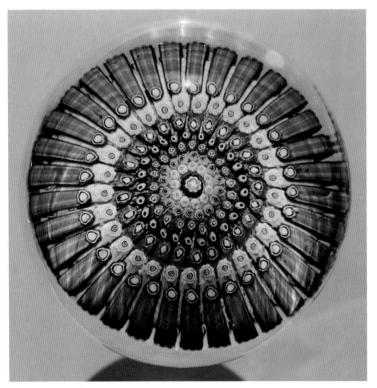

Whitefriars magnum seven row concentric paperweight, c. 1950. Dia. 4", Height 2.4". *Author's collection.* $500/750.
This is an early paperweight by Whitefriars, probably made around the late 1950s. The canes are tightly packed together which has resulted in a little squashing and distortion, but otherwise a rare magnum example from this famous glassworks.

Whitefriars black swan paperweight. Dia. 3", Height 2.1". *Private collection.* **$1,500/2,000.**
This is a very rare commission piece for the Western Australia company Myers. The piece was produced in a limited edition of 50 for the 150th anniversary of the State. The rare motifs made by Whitefriars are now commanding very significant prices that are related to the scarcity and number produced. Often a limited edition would not be totally subscribed, and as an example, the partridge Christmas weight had an edition of 1000, but only 593 were ever produced.

Whitefriars 1979 star pattern paperweight. Dia. 3", Height 2.2". *Courtesy of a private collection.* **$750/1,000.**
This is a very rare star pattern on a black ground which has a multitude of complex canes in green, yellow, pink, and white softly colored canes. The central feature cane is itself a very complex five row concentric cane that would make a good weight if enlarged to full size. This cane makes this paperweight a very rare and unusual Whitefriars piece.

Whitefriars 1977 commemorative paperweight. Dia. 3", Height 2.1". *Author's collection.* **$450/600.**
This commemorative paperweight was produced in 1977 in an edition of 1000 of which all were taken up. The ribbon twists are a little different and rarely found in Whitefriar paperweights.

Whitefriars 1978 large butterfly paperweight. Dia. 3", Height 2.1". *Peter Hall collection.* **$1,000/1,200.**
This butterfly is the larger version of three types made by Whitefriars and as such would usually command a price at auction 30% higher than the other two. Many of the butterflies, birds, fish, etc., made as large motifs such as this have risen dramatically in price over the past five years as collectors have realized that although the piece may not be a limited edition, very few were actually made. In some cases only fifty of sixty were produced in a limited edition of one hundred.

Whitefriars 1980 large bell paperweight. Dia. 3", Height 2.2".
Author's collection. $900/1,200.
This bell made from tiny millefiori canes is set with spaced canes and a garland over a dark blue ground. The edition size was scheduled to be one thousand and was issued to catch the Christmas trade, but only two hundred and fifty eight were made and sold before the company closed in the same year.

Whitefriars fish paperweight in close up. Dia. 3", Height 2.2".
Author's collection. $1,000/1,200.
This close up view of a central motif used by Whitefriars allows one to see the dexterity and enormous attention to detail that the setters have achieved in the creation of these micro-mosaic pictures in glass. This fish weight is quite rare and was made in an unlimited number, but very few were made, possibly only several hundred estimated from the amount that are known to collectors.

Whitefriars 1979 partridge in a pear tree paperweight. Dia. 3", Height 2.2". *Author's collection.* $1,200/1,700.
The partridge weight has an amazing number of tiny colored rods in each element of the design: in this piece a single pear has well over a hundred rods in each fruit and approximately hundred pears and leaves. The canes and rods used in this weight have been calculated precisely by Roy Brown, the English collector with an appreciation for millefiori canes to 9,469 rods. It is not surprising the Whitefriars weights are now so coveted by collectors worldwide. The edition size was intended to be one thousand, but only five hundred and ninety three were made.

Whitefriars 1975 garland of angels paperweight. Dia. 3", Height 2.2". *Courtesy of Hannah, Sophie, Bethany and Charles Hall.* $650/850.
This lovely Christmas weight has a delightful garland of angels on a dark blue ground, all set around a large blue and white angel on a white tablet. After a number of years trying to buy one of these angel weights for each of my grandchildren, I have finally made it and will be presenting each with their first Whitefriars paperweight. Eventually, I hope this will help them to start their own collections.

**Whitefriars 1977 manger and angels paperweight. Dia. 3",
Height 2.2".** *Author's collection.* **$650/850.**
This Christmas, limited edition of one thousand was not fully subscribed and only seven hundred and thirty eight were made. A host of
angels fly over the cattle shed and manger in this nativity scene.

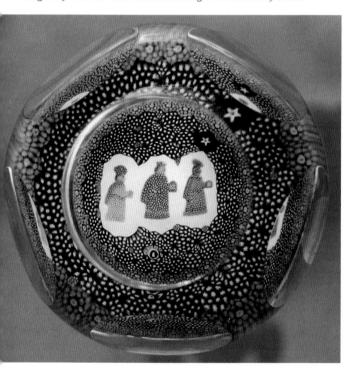

**Whitefriars 1976 three wise men paperweight. Dia. 3", Height
2.2".** *Author's collection.* **$650/850.**
Issued in an edition of one thousand, only nine hundred and one were
recorded in the factory records as being made for the Christmas trade in
1976. The bundling of rods to make figures and fauna was the closest the
company came to lampworking, which technically it isn't, but it is creative
in the lampwork style.

Right:
**Whitefriars 1977 five Liberty bells paperweight. Dia. 3", Height
2.2".** *Private collection.* **$1,000/1,500.**
Five radiating latticinio twists separate the five bells in this very rare
Whitefriars limited edition that was destined to be sold in the USA only.
The edition was only one hundred of which fifty seven were made. This
production of 57 paperweights probably makes this piece the rarest of all
the Whitefriars paperweights, with the exception of the one-off test pieces,
and would be hotly contested at auction if collectors knew of the very small
numbers produced.

**Whitefriars 1976 US flag, bell, and eagle in a garland
paperweight. Dia. 3", Height 2.2".** *Private collection.*
$1,000/1,500.
At this point in time, I have not seen one of these weights at auction,
so it is a guess as to how much it would achieve. The weight was a
limited edition of one hundred but only sixty nine were made, a fact
that makes this example one of the most sought after paperweights
made by Whitefriars. The USA collection pieces are rarely seen in
the UK and would be keenly contested at auction by the growing
fraternity of Whitefriar lovers. The symbolic eagle, bell, and flag are
set within a blue and white garland on a dark blue ground. The
weights were boxed with a certificate of authenticity.

Whitefriars 1977 three flags paperweight. Dia. 3", Height 2.2".
Private collection. **$850/1,000.**
Another rare limited edition of five hundred, of which only one hundred and ninety four were made.

Whitefriars 1977 wine decanter. Height 8.5". *Author's collection.* **$850/1,000.**
This is a beautifully cut decanter with a paperweight stopper. It was made as a limited edition of only fifty, but several other decanters were also made with a different millefiori pattern for the stopper. I do not know the total output of these decanters, but it was certainly not many judging by their scarcity in the market place. A nice piece which I use often.

Below:
Whitefriars ashtrays. Dia. 4". *Author's collection.* **$250/300 each.**
Despite branching out into other items with millefiori inclusions, such as these ashtrays, the order book for 1980 was not enough to sustain trading. After the last trade fair in August of 1979, which did not generate enough orders to allow the company to trade within the insolvency laws, the directors decided to allow in the government receivers to try and sell the business as a going concern, in order to preserve the very talented workforce. Unable to find a buyer for the business in the time allowed, the assets were sold to the highest bidder, Caithness Glass.

Whitefriars 1976 four eagles paperweight. Dia. 3", Height 2.2". *Private collection.* **$850/1,000.**
A rare limited edition of one hundred, of which only seventy were made. The Whitefriars company records are held by Caithness Glass Limited, who bought the name and assets of the bankrupt company in 1980.

American Paperweights

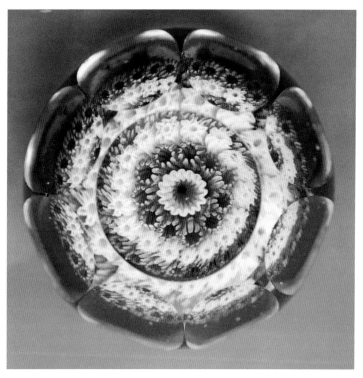

The inspiration and many skills involved in paperweight making were almost certainly brought across the Atlantic by immigrant workers seeking a new life in the USA. Many of the immigrants were glassworkers from factories in Europe, such as Bacchus of Birmingham where paperweight maker William Gillinder had worked before setting off to America in 1854. He began work at the New England Glassworks (NEGC), and later established his own company called the Philadelphia Flint Glassworks. Another migrant named Nicholas Lutz had worked at the Saint Louis glassworks in France before emigrating to America and joining the Sandwich Glass Company.

Both of these men are thought to have taken glass canes with them to America as weights have been found with silhouette canes of Queen Victoria identical to silhouettes found in Bacchus weights of the same period. Similarly, Saint Louis canes can be seen in Sandwich paperweights. Contributions to American antique paperweights must have come from the numerous migrants who traveled from all over Europe in their quest for a better lifestyle. The European styles for paperweights dominated the American production of the 1850s, with very little innovation from the established patterns and set ups recognizable as European. Many American businessmen and visitors could have returned with samples of paperweights from one of the many European glass and industry exhibitions that were being held throughout Europe at this time, including the Crystal Palace Exhibition of 1851, when several paperweight makers displayed their wares, including Bacchus of Birmingham.

Production of glass paperweights continued, sporadically, to the early part of the twentieth century, when it seems that almost every glasshouse in the USA had begun turning out paperweights, usually as frits or end of the day weights as gifts for family and friends. Most of these weights are simply made with spattered grounds and few have millefiori canes, but some were dated and signed with names of the recipient (i.e. Mother) or with advertisements. These early designs within the glass were usually of simple flowers made from picking up powdered glass; but, as skills developed, crimping tools and dies were used by many glassworkers to create roses, lilies, and many other flowers.

The works of many important American paperweight makers from the turn of the twentieth century have been well documented with photographs and stories of the makers, in the definitive book on the subject by Jean S. Melvin, *American Glass Paperweights and Their Makers* published by Thomas Nelson, New York. Although last printed in 1970, the book should still be available on request from a good lending library, and should be considered a must for the serious student of early American paperweight makers. As for the antique American paperweights, the book written by Paul Hollister, Jr. *The Encyclopaedia of Glass Paperweights*, published by Paperweight Press, Locust Street, Santa Cruz, California, contains detailed histories and identity clues in American antique paperweights made by the two main antique paperweight glass factories, The New England Glass Company and The Sandwich Glass Company. As a general guide to identifying the main

William T. Gillinder faceted concentric paperweight, c. 1850. Dia. 2.9", Height 1.75". *Courtesy of Gary and Marge McClanahan.* $6,000/8,000.

This is a very typical Gillinder paperweight. Many of the weights attributable to this glassworks can be very similar in design. In some paperweights, Gillinder used the same type of canes to create carpet grounds of color. Even when all white canes were used to create a carpet ground, with the addition of a central cane of a pastel color, the result is still a stunning paperweight. White ruffle canes were a favorite of the factory and have been used in many paperweights. Sometimes a row of colored canes could be inserted or just a single large central cane of a different color. This example has eight facets with a large window on the top to view the interior. The canes in this weight are softly colored with an open pale yellow cane in the center. Many of the canes used by Gillinder reflect his time at the Bacchus glassworks in England. The use of pastel colors and open ruffle canes are very much in the style of George Bacchus & Company.

Side view of William T. Gillinder faceted paperweight.
This view shows another Bacchus feature, which is the pulling down and drawing to the underneath of the weight of the outside row of canes. This finishes and tidies the base, which has been ground to a shallow concavity.

differences of the two companies' weights, the NEGC paperweights have a much higher profile and are heavier in the hand as against the Sandwich paperweights, which usually have a low profile and are much lighter in the hand as very little lead was added to their glass compounds.

Today's contemporary American makers are the creators of artistic paperweights with a content that has surpassed even the antique French makers of the classic period. Most of the current paperweight makers take their inspiration from the works of Charles Kaziun, Harold Hacker, and a few other pioneers of paperweight making in the classic style. Kaziun, for instance, is regarded as one of the twentieth century's greatest paperweight makers. Kaziun created works with flowers, reptiles, and millefiori designs which may be overlaid by up to three different colors to encase the set ups. Kaziun has been inspirational for many of today's individual makers. Today's modern paperweight makers may be working from small glass shops or a lone worker may be creating weights at home in the basement or garage. As the lone workers have become well known, they have expanded their operations to small, custom built units in the back yard, but they are still working alone with the occasional helping hand from wife or husband.

Sandwich Glass Company dahlia flower paperweight, c. 1850. Dia. 2.8", Height 1.75" *Courtesy of Gary and Marge McClanahan.* **$1,000/1,400.**
A dahlia flower with a green and white outer layer, and pink canes bunched together around a small millefiori central cane. The inner petals are rods of clear glass with an outer layer of pink which have been collapsed to form elongated tubes that resemble the curved almost circular petals in a dahlia flower head.

New England Glass Company pears and cherries over latticinio, c. 1850. Dia. 2.9", Height 1.9". *Courtesy of Gary and Marge McClanahan.* **$800/1,000.**
The precise and geometrical arrangements of this fruit weight are pretty typical of paperweights from the New England and Sandwich glass factories. This example is well made over a very precise latticinio basket. Although a good American antique example, this paperweight would not quite achieve the price of the Saint Louis equivalent. As an example based on current prices (2000), the French version would be around $1,200/1,500.

New England Glass Company blown apple paperweight, c. 1850. Diameter of base 3", Height 2.75". *Courtesy of Gary and Marge McClanahan.* **$1,000/1,500.**
This apple sits on a base that is usually described as a "cookie base." The beautifully blended and subtle colors would seem more appropriate to a peach than an apple in this very desirable and different paperweight.

Sandwich Glass Company buttercup paperweight, c. 1850. Dia. 2.9", Height 1.75". *Courtesy of Gary and Marge McClanahan.* **$2,000/2,400.**

This is a striking example of a flower weight with an excellent combination of colors. The large white buttercup has a hint of yellow around a layer of petals near the center of the flower. The flattened outer petals are backed by five dark green leaves. The whole flower is set on a red jasper ground that frames the set up beautifully.

New England Glass Company cruciform paperweight, c. 1850. Dia. 3.25", Height 2.2". *Courtesy of Gary and Marge McClanahan.* **$4,000/5,000.**

This very precisely made buttercup yellow cruciform has been constructed from lampworked leaves of identical size which have been fused together and then laid centrally over spiraling latticinio of the highest quality. The central millefiori cane in blue and white compliments the yellow of the leaves. This paperweight displays many of the precise construction qualities associated with the NEGC.

Sandwich Glass Company cruciform paperweight, c. 1850. Dia. 3", Height 1.9". *Courtesy of Gary and Marge McClanahan.* **$600/800.**

A cruciform of millefiori canes, set over clear glass in red and blue with two nice leaves attached to the stem in this symbolic design.

New England Glass Company concentric paperweight, c. 1850. Dia. 2.75", Height 1.9". *Courtesy of Gary and Marge McClanahan.* **$700/900.**

This is a very fine NEGC weight with two rows of complex millefiori canes and a row of white spaced canes set around a central cane which has a small running rabbit or hare, in white on a black base. The whole set up has been laid over a nice white latticinio spiral.

New England Glass Company two row concentric with central clematis and leaves, c. 1850. Dia. 2.7", Height 1.75". *Courtesy of Gary and Marge McClanahan.* **$2,200/2,500.**

This is quite a rare example with the red clematis and dark green leaves sitting over a bed of spiraling latticinio. Two rows of complex canes frame the nicely made flower.

Side view of nosegay paperweight.

The side view shows the canes drawn down to the base of the weight with very little tapering to the stem. The French Baccarat and Saint Louis makers usually drew their canes down to a very thin taper with the mushroom stem thinning out to a matchstick size where it meets the base. The thickness of this mushroom stalk adds interest as the millefiori canes can be seen in some detail.

New England Glass Company nosegay paperweight, c. 1850. Dia. 3", Height 2.2". *Courtesy of Gary and Marge McClanahan.* **$3,000/3,500.**

A rare mushroom and nosegay paperweight within three rows of complex canes. The nosegay, with three or four leaves and three flower heads, was a favorite and quite common design that was made in considerable quantities at the French glassworks of Saint Louis. Many foreign glassworkers were employed by the two biggest producers of paperweights in this area along the east coast of America, in the nineteenth century. The workers had come from Baccarat, Murano, and Bohemia to offer their skills learned in the "old world."

Base view of nosegay paperweight.

The basal view is an attractive feature in this rare weight. With the canes drawn down without a significant taper, it allows one to look inside the interior to the lampworked flower arrangement on the top of the weight.

New England Glass Company four row concentric paperweight, c. 1850. Dia. 2.8", Height 1.9". *Courtesy of Gary and Marge McClanahan.* **$2,000/2,500.**

An extremely fine and rare concentric paperweight that matches the finest antique concentric weights from the great glassworks of Europe. Precisely made concentrics were achieved especially by Saint Louis and this example could easily be mistaken for one of the fine weights made in France. The complex canes in blue, white orange, and biscuit color are neatly set around a complex large central feature cane.

New England Glass Company upright bouquet paperweight, c. 1850. Dia. 3", Height 2.2". *Courtesy of Gary and Marge McClanahan.* **$1,600/2,000.**

Six individual flowers surround a very complex central millefiori cane, which makes a fine display in this rare bouquet from NEGC. The bouquet sits over a spiral latticinio ground, beautifully made and centralized. The weight has six sides and a large top facet, each facet separated by a long vertical cut. This weight could have been made by a worker trained at Saint Louis as it is similar in style and coloring to fine Saint Louis pieces.

New England Glass Company patterned paperweight, c. 1850. Dia. 2.8", Height 1.9". *Courtesy of Gary and Marge McClanahan.* **$600/800.**

A patterned paperweight with the design incorporating biscuit colored canes similar to the previous weight. This patterned design is not as neatly set as in other simple concentrics, as this weight shows misaligned millefiori canes that are in unequal numbers within the pattern, varying from two to three canes in a row. This makes me think that the canes were set out free hand and not in a die, as most concentrics would have been to achieve the precision required. The weight also has a latticinio bed which is untidily made and which would indicate a weight made by an apprentice or new worker.

Rare Sandwich Glass Company poinsettia paperweight, c. 1850. Dia. 2.75", Height 1.7". *Courtesy of Gary and Marge McClanahan.* **$1,800/2,000.**

A simple but beautifully executed five leaf poinsettia set above a ground of orange chippings. The veins in the leaves are very detailed and considerable skill and care must have been taken in this lampwork exercise. Many of the finer paperweights that have come from the Sandwich glasshouse have been accredited to Nicholas Lutz during his time with this glasshouse. He worked there from 1869 to 1888 when the factory was forced to close. Lutz had previously worked at the NEGC.

103

Sandwich Glass Company blue poinsettia paperweight, c. 1850. Dia. 2.7", Height 1.6". *Courtesy of Gary and Marge McClanahan.* **$1,100/1,400.**

Sandwich produced many poinsettia weights, with blue and red being the most common. This type of poinsettia weight can be found on clear, or with a latticinio backing, and on a spattered ground as in this example. The backing leaves are deeply veined in dark green glass. The central canes are usually complex or have a feature such as arrowheads.

Sandwich Glass Company white poinsettia, c. 1850. Dia. 2.75", Height 1.7". *Courtesy of Gary and Marge McClanahan.* **$1,200/1,800.**

A very nice and rare poinsettia with white petals dotted with aventurine/goldstone. The quality of this weight is superb compared with some Sandwich examples, which can be loosely put together. This piece was probably made by Nicholas Lutz, because of his penchant for using goldstone, which he had learned to use during his days working in Murano, Italy, where goldstone was extensively used in paperweights and many other household and decorative items. The leaves in this weight are also dotted deliberately with small bubbles, a feature which can be seen on many poinsettia paperweights.

Side view of Sandwich Glass Company blue poinsettia paperweight.

Sandwich paperweights usually show a low profile in comparison to the New England Glass Company weights. In this weight we can see that the dome is cushion shaped with the flower set high in the dome of glass.

Sandwich Glass Company scrambled paperweight, c. 1850. Dia. 2.9", Height 1.7". *Courtesy of Gary and Marge McClanahan.* **$350/600.**

Scrambled paperweights are normally the result of the end of the day's unused whole canes and chipped canes, although in this nice example the canes are in an unusually good condition. These weights are inexpensive to buy but can be a very useful aid in identification because of the great variety of canes usually found inside. The low dome and muted colors are normally attributed to Sandwich, but, as the NEGC factory was close by, a certain amount of cane exchanges must have taken place between workers, as identical canes are occasionally found in each company's paperweights.

New England Glass Company scrambled paperweight, c. 1850. Dia. 3", Height 1.9". *Courtesy of Gary and Marge McClanahan.* $500/700.
This scrambled weight from NEGC has an array of much brighter and more colorful canes than the previous example from neighboring Sandwich. The scrambled European version from Clichy and Saint Louis are very similar in content and sizes to the American and the factories' products are often confused with each others.

New England Glass Company crown paperweight, c. 1850. Dia. 2.7", Height 1.7". *Courtesy of Gary and Marge McClanahan.* $1,200/1,500.
Over twenty strands of twisted colored rods are used to create this crown. The very colorful twists are in two or three colorways, including: red, white, and a canary yellow; blue, white, and yellow; and blue and white.

New England Glass Company crown paperweight, c. 1850. Dia. 2.7", Height 1.7". *Courtesy of Gary and Marge McClanahan.* $1,500/2,000.
Most American crown weights were made by the NEGC, but Sandwich also made a few which are slightly inferior to the quality achieved by their rivals at the NEGC. Therefore, Sandwich did not pursue this product style in any great numbers. This weight has strongly colored strands of twisted glass in a multitude of color combinations, all radiating from the large central feature cane. This weight also has facets cut on six sides with a window on top.

New England Glass Company crown paperweight, c. 1850. Dia. 2.7", Height 1.7". *Courtesy of Gary and Marge McClanahan.* $1,500/2,000.
This crown weight has a combination of five different spiral rods set around a large white central feature cane. The twisted rods are made in strongly colored reds, green, black, blue, and yellow, interspersed with a red, white, and blue filigree cane.

105

Sandwich Glass Company poinsettia paperweight, c. 1850. Dia. 2.9", Height 1.8". *Author's collection.* **$800/1,000.**
This is my only antique American paperweight, bought by mistake from Paul Ysart's financial backer Robert Gunn during an interview with him in 1998. I saw the paperweight in Gunn's display cabinet among his Harland glass paperweight collection and recognized the arrowhead canes as being by Saint Louis. As Gunn was selling the last remnants of the Ysart stock he had acquired on the closure of the premises, he was willing to sell the weight. Only on careful examination later did I realize that the weight was a Sandwich Glass Company paperweight with a Saint Louis arrowhead cane set in the center. A good example of millefiori canes *traveling* between different manufacturers and continents. The weight is a beautifully made piece, with small bubbles set among the petals as dew-drops. Originally bought from a London auction by Graham Brown, who was sales manager for Harland Glass, with the idea that Paul Ysart could use the weight as an example of antique, French lampwork.

Close-up of arrow cane.
The rounded end of the arrowhead is also known as an anchor cane, which has also been found in antique Bohemian paperweights to confuse us even further.
Contemporary American lampworked paperweights and their makers have arguably reached a standard of excellence that surpasses the French and English antiques in terms of content, glass clarity, and lampwork.
Although small in numbers, the American artists, working from small glass shops which are sometimes at home in the basement or garage, are creating weights that are eagerly bought by enthusiastic collectors worldwide.
Many museums around the world now showcase American paperweights alongside nineteenth century classic paperweights from the 1845-1852 era.
Many American weights are made in a classical style: creating reproductions of the pansy, rose, and most of the flowers used by their French counterparts of the nineteenth century. The American artists have expanded on these themes to create work that is almost botanically perfect in the construction and coloring of their floral weights. Many artists have also reproduced snakes and lizards, birds and butterflies, fruit and insects in life-like representations of the

flora and fauna they view around them. Other artists have concentrated on millefiori subjects and are presenting collectors of fine paperweights with a variety of weights that are set as precisely as the best of the French and English antique paperweights. American paperweight makers are few in number and widely spread across the country, with a small knot of glasshouses based on the west coast and a few more concentrated on the east coast. The workshops in which they create their paperweights will usually have just one or two workers, and it is from these very specialized studio type glasshouses that the superior examples of this art form are originating. Prices for American contemporary paperweights are reflected in the amount of work involved in the creation of each unique piece. Even at auction, paperweights of just a few years of age are fetching premium prices because of the low production of these artists. It is not unusual for a studio to produce as few as one or two weights per week.

Drew Ebelhare millefiori cross paperweight. Approx. 3" dia.
Courtesy of Gary and Marge McClanahan. **$650/850.**
This millefiori cross weight has a wide and varied selection of colorful
canes. The cross is formed with lovely pink and blue complex canes and a
yellow center. Although at first glance, the four panels appear to be close
packed random canes, a closer inspection reveals that the panels opposite
each other are in fact almost a mirror image. The whole set up is centered
perfectly within the dome of encapsulating glass with the outer row of pink
and white solid rod canes drawn beneath the weight to form a basket.
There are not many American artists pursuing millefiori designs because of
the very expensive and time consuming work creating the canes and as a
single person workshop, the drawing of the canes can be a problem. It is
not possible to show, within the confines of this book, an example of
paperweights from every artist, but the following paperweights are a good
representative selection of the work currently being produced in the USA.

**Gordon Smith and James Kontes 1994 peaches paperweight. Approx.
3".** *Courtesy of Gary and Marge McClanahan.* **$1,400/1,800.**
This collaborative paperweight has everything the collector wants in a paperweight, it has realistically colored fruits with a peach fuzz to the skin, three
unopened flower buds, and a central fully open, pink peach flower blossom,
with a very delicately made yellow stamen. The arrangement sits over six perfect
leaves and, to cap it all, the whole arrangement is encircled with a beautiful pink
and white torsade. The artistry of the two men involved in the making of this
piece is perfection personified.

**Bob Banford magnum strawberries and blossom
paperweight.** *Author's collection.* **Dia. 3.6".**
$1,800/2,200.
This is a very fine and realistic interpretation of a
strawberry plant in all stages of producing the fruit.
Perfect white flowers with a half ripened fruit next to three
fully ripened and good enough to eat red berries.
Attention to detail is the main criteria that decides
whether the recreation in glass of a strawberry plant is
perfect or just *representative*. Here Bob Banford has
created a paperweight that even the most discerning
collector would revere. The whole set up is beautifully
centered over a white latticinio ground that frames the
strawberries perfectly.

Francis Whittemore nosegay paperweight. Approx. Dia. 2.7".
Courtesy of Gary and Marge McClanahan. $400/600.
Four millefiori canes sit prettily on a background of five leaves. The nosegay paperweight design was a favorite of both the Saint Louis glassworks and their American counterpart, the New England Glass Company. Now we have another generation using the same design to great effect. This nosegay rests on a ground of white glass to make the style a little different from its predecessors.

Nantes Kontes vegetable paperweight. Approx. Dia. 3". *Courtesy of Gary and Marge McClanahan. $750/1,000.*
Aubergines, carrots, two radishes with leaves, and a signature NK in yellow on a leaf. This creation is very realistic, the aubergines are beautiful and realistically colored. The formation of the leaves attached to the aubergine fruit are also very natural in appearance. The whole arrangement is set above a lacy latticinio bed with a pink and white torsade around the outer edge of the weight.

Francis Whittemore crimped rose paperweight. Approx. Dia. 2.5". *Courtesy of Gary and Marge McClanahan. $300/500.*
A stunning multi petaled yellow rose, made with the aid of a crimping tool, makes this weight stand out from the crowd. The deep buttercup yellow rose sits above a bed of green leaves with the set up in a clear glass ball which is then seated on a pedestal in the Millville fashion.

Ken Rosenfeld 1987 rose paperweight. Dia. 3.25", Height 2.4". *Courtesy of Gary and Marge McClanahan. $750/1,000.*
A stunning arrangement of petals in this pink cabbage rose makes for a fine central feature and, when surrounded by two rows of pure white and deep royal blue flowers, it makes this a fine example from this wonderful artist. Each of the blue flowers has a set of green leaves beneath the flower head and the whole piece is set on clear glass.

Mayuel Ward butterfly and flowers paperweight. Dia. 3.25", Height 2.6". *Author's collection.* **$750/1,000.**
A monarch butterfly hovers above the arrangement, deciding which flower to settle on first. The lovely flowers in this weight are backed with leaves and all set over clear glass. Mayuel Ward worked for the Abelman Art Glass studio but now works alone to produce these fine weights which are all of collector quality and a joy to behold. As with many American contemporary makers, Mayuel now signs his paperweights by etching on the outside of the glass to prevent any signature cane interfering with the aesthetic look of a piece.

Rick Ayotte magnum daisies and blueberries paperweight. Dia. 4.25", Height 2.75". *Author's collection.* **$1,800/2,200.**
Amazing life-like blueberries with a bloom on the skin that gives the berries a look that must have taken a long time to perfect. I have asked Rick how he achieves this bloom and, with a wagging finger to his nose, he politely declines to tell me. The techniques used in creating this paperweight are many and varied and remain a secret to the artist, just like his glassworker predecessors from the distant past, who were threatened with death should they divulge glassmaking secrets to outsiders. The three daisies are colored in a light pastel pink, pale blue and off white, with the arrangement set on a bed of green and brown leaves. Like many American artists, Ayotte makes his paperweights using slugs of optically clear glass, which gives American weights a little extra clarity compared to European examples.

Paul Stankard 1986 trailing arbutus with root people paperweight. Approx. Dia. 3.5". *Courtesy of Gary and Marge McClanahan.* **$5,000/7,500.**

Paul Stankards paperweights usually attract high prices at retail and auctions because he is generally recognized as the most accurate and botanically correct artist at present making paperweights. This arbutus pink flower with its trailing leaves and roots, is as near perfect a representation of the flower as you can get, even down to the spotting and discoloration on the leaves. This paperweight demonstrates artistry, a botanists eye, and a knowledge of glass making at its best.

Left:
Base view of Paul Stankard paperweight.
The base view shows four root or spirit people clinging to the realistic roots of the plant. These miniature people are no more than 3 or 4 centimeters in size. The roots are revealed as though they were water plants in an aquarium, which makes the base as fascinating as the top of the weight.

Right:
Ken Rosenfeld mixed flower arrangement. Dia. 3.25", Height 2.4". *Author's collection.* **$600/800.**

This flower collection is of the highest quality workmanship and it makes one wonder how the artist can progress from perfection already achieved. This piece of *museum quality* was commissioned by the author on Ken Rosenfelds recent visit to the UK. He gave a lecture at the Cambridge Paperweight Circle in Cambridge, England, where his display of paperweights for sale after the lecture had sold out by the time I managed to get to the front of the line. Ken said he would make and send me a paperweight when he got back to the US. This is the result of his efforts on my behalf, a wonderful lampwork paperweight.

Val-Saint-Lambert Paperweights

There must have been many countries throughout Europe whose glass industries have produced paperweights over the last 150 years or so and many European glassworks established in the eighteenth and nineteenth centuries are still in existence to this day. A great interchange of workers and ideas had begun after the Venetians realized they could not prevent forever the secrets, they had pioneered in glass from escaping the island of Murano, where their glass industry had been concentrated. It was these migrant glassworkers that spread the once secret techniques far and wide to secure better conditions and lives for their families.

Although paperweights have not emerged in any great numbers to signify a major production run, paperweights have been traced back to the Val-Saint-Lambert crystal works in Belgium in sufficient numbers to suggest that the company produced paperweights in the nineteenth century to satisfy their own domestic markets. Having collected paperweights for nearly thirty years, my experience with Val-Saint-Lambert paperweights would indicate that for every 300 or so French and English weights that appear at auction, one Belgium weight might be encountered. It would also appear that more turn up in American auctions than European, which suggests that some were taken by immigrants or perhaps a small amount were exported by the company.

Many odd weights, usually containing bubbles over a spattered ground of melted glass chippings, do turn up quite regularly in English and European antiques fairs and flea markets and sometimes these are attributed to the other glass producers of the region, Verrerie Bougard and Verrerie Nationales, but could have been made by almost any European glassmaker, this type of paperweight is widespread and was probably made as an end of day weight by the glassworker as presents and gifts for the family.

The Val-Saint-Lambert crystal works was founded by Francois Kemlin and Auguste Lelievre, with the aid of a financial group, in 1825. The new company was based in the old abbey of Rosieres, Val-Saint-Lambert in the town of Seraing. The abandoned Cistercian monastery was chosen because of its closeness to the Meuse river and the vast Belgium coalfields needed to fuel its furnaces. Today's modern glassworks has a large visitor center with a capacity of 200,000 persons a year and produces glassware that is exported worldwide. Paperweights are still produced but do not include lampwork or millefiori canes and are of the abstract type. The company also boasts a museum which unfortunately does not have any of its own antique paperweights on display.

Val-Saint-Lambert vermilion flower with torsade, c. 1850. Dia. 2.8". *Collection of Karen and Paul Dunlop. Photo ©2000 Papier Presse.* $4,000/5,000.
A simple red flower with six petals around an unusual hollow cogged millefiori cane for its center. The lightly patterned leaves and petals are beautifully made in a style very similar to antique Baccarat paperweights. The flower has a blue and pink torsade around the edge to frame the piece perfectly. Although the piece appears to be quite simple, the rarity of Val-Saint-Lambert paperweights guarantees a substantial premium at auction over similar Baccarat antiques.

Val-Saint-Lambert pansy on blue ground with torsade, c. 1850. Dia. 3.6". *Collection of Karen and Paul Dunlop. Photo ©2000 Papier Presse.* $800/1,200.
A striking blue ground highlights this pansy with two leaves and a three color torsade on the edge of the paperweight. At over three and a half inches in diameter, the weight should be considered as a magnum.

Val-Saint-Lambert double pansy on a mica ground, c. 1870. Dia. 3.6". Collection of Karen and Paul Dunlop. Photo ©2000 Papier Presse. $2,000/3,000.
A double headed pansy paperweight without a torsade. Many of the Val-Saint-Lambert weights have a torsade, which is almost a trademark recognition feature. The flowers are set over a mica ground which became very fashionable in many Bohemian glass objects towards the end of the nineteenth century and this suggests that this piece was made after c. 1870.

Val-Saint-Lambert "14" paperweight, c. 1850. Dia. 3.3". Collection of Karen and Paul Dunlop. Photo ©2000 Papier Presse. $1,200/1,500.
An unusual paperweight that appears to be a commission piece or frit, perhaps for a birthday, and made by the father? The paperweight has a tree with white flowers and leaves which have been carelessly attached. The whole design is fanciful and was surely intended as a gift. The blue ground and torsade has been constructed with precision.

Val-Saint-Lambert striped flower with torsade, c. 1850. Dia. 2.9". Collection of Karen and Paul Dunlop. Photo ©2000 Papier Presse. $8,000/10,000.
This is a very rare flower design, created with the aid of small steel picks and tweezers which manipulate the hot glass at the lamp to make the stripes. The petals are made from the same cane rod as the outer torsade. The base is star cut in this very beautiful flower paperweight.

Val-Saint-Lambert monogrammed magnum paperweight with torsade, c. 1850. Dia. 3.9". Collection of Karen and Paul Dunlop. Photo ©2000 Papier Presse. $1,800/2,000.
The monogram is engraved on a dark plaque before being inserted within the dome of glass. The weight has a bright yellow ground with a decoration of millefiori canes. Made as a frit or commission to be presented to M.R?

Russian Paperweights

Paperweights and plaques that are now thought to have been made in Russian glassworks are usually constructed with magnificent lampworked bouquets of flowers. Previously many of these floral weights and plaques were thought to have been made by the Mount Washington glassworks in the USA. These paperweights must have been made in very small quantities due to the extreme rarity of the pieces. The 1999 sale of the Friedrich Bader collection of paperweights in Vienna, Austria, included many seals, plaques and paperweights with almost identical composition and coloring to the Mount Washington pieces. Most of the Bader floral plaques and paperweights have been found in Russia and other eastern European states, so it would seem to indicate that this region is a likely source of these fine weights and lampworked objects. Several pieces can be traced to a family with links to the glass industry in the Minsk area of Russia, but further research is required to pinpoint the glassworks. Occasionally, a lampworked caterpillar or butterfly has been added as an extra display of the artist's skill and dexterity at the lamp.

Consideration of the design and manufacturing complexities of these glass masterpieces would seem to indicate that the paperweights and plaques, sometimes with a matching seal, were made as a gift or commission. No paperweights have appeared that are of a lower quality which would suggest a mass produced item. These glass paperweights and other lampworked objects would have been an expensive item to acquire in nineteenth century Russia, and would be in the sole domain of the aristocracy and rich merchants.

The history of Russian glass goes way back in time to around the tenth century to small items of colored glass, such as beads and simple jewelry, which have been found on archaeological sites; but, this fledgling glass industry floundered under the rule of the conquering Mongol armies of occupation. In the fifteenth century, once free from foreign rule, Russia began to get its glass industries organized. By the time we get to the early nineteenth century, the Russian glass industry was given a huge boost when the government banned the import of foreign glass. Glassmaking became a major industry with nearly 150 glassworks employing many thousands of workers in and around the main population centers. With a plentiful supply of raw materials and a protectionism policy in place, business flourished and areas such as St. Petersburg could boast as many as 14 large glassworks on its doorstep.

It was quite usual for the owners of important glassworks to attend exhibitions and trade shows abroad, where they could purchase samples of foreign products that could be copied and used on the domestic market. It would be reasonable to assume, that with the close cultural and business links between the French and Russians around this time, that paperweights and lampworked pieces were brought home from these trips abroad. French was widely spoken at this time by the Russian aristocracy, and it was commonplace for workers from foreign countries to be brought in to teach the local workforce the mysteries of glassmaking, with a long term aim for them to become self sufficient in skill and designs. It was noted also, in the well documented company records of some of the glassworks, that the best of the glassmakers were sent abroad to improve on their skills, returning later with new techniques and the latest trends and ideas. The senior glass artists in the glassworks also were encouraged to go abroad to visit exhibitions, etc., and to purchase specimens of foreign items that could be utilized by the factory. Many of the bigger glassworks, such as the Imperial Glassworks, near St. Petersburg, exhibited at many foreign venues; for example, the 1862 London world's fair in England. By the late 1800s, Russia had become a major glassmaking country with over two hundred and seventy glassworks in fifty provinces.

Paperweights from Russia are extremely rare and very valuable and many reside in the collections of museums. However, The Vienna Art Auctions, Palais Kinsky, Vienna, Austria, have kindly allowed the reproduction of catalogue illustrations of the Friedrich Bader paperweight collection, as offered for auction in December 1999, as examples of these fabulous objects.

The collection was built up by Friederich Bader and his past family over three generations of collecting. At one time they had a collection of 3000 paperweights and related objects. Twelve years ago, Frederich Bader started to specialize in Russian pieces and gradually reduced his collection and enhanced its value. Having established the finest collection of Russian pieces in the world, achieved with the help of up to five hundred people scouring antique shops and markets in eastern European countries, he was able to make comparisons with the weights and plaques attributed to the Mount Washington Glassworks and his own Russian pieces. He theorizes that a client of the glassworks would commission a seal and a matching paperweight at the same time; this is verified by matching pieces within his own collection. Cyrillic engravings on the paperweights also points to a Russian attribution, but alas, not to a named factory. These lampworked pieces are thought to have been made at any time during the second half of the nineteenth century.

Seals with strawberries and bouquet in each. Height 3.75". *Courtesy of The Vienna Art Auctions, Palais Kinsky, Vienna, Austria.* **$5,000/7,500.**

Very beautiful seals with overlaid white and red strawberries in each, with bouquets of blooms that look like passion flowers. The seals are cut in a drop shape and have engraving to the bases that indicates these objects were intended for use as seals and not just as decoration. The glass is much lighter than the French crystal and is very clear.

Russian seals with lampwork. Approx. height 2.75". *Courtesy of The Vienna Art Auctions, Palais Kinsky, Vienna, Austria. $2,000/3,500 each.*
Various colored dahlia flowers in each of the seals that have all been made at the lamp. The piece on the left has a name in Cyrillic lettering on the base which is held in a brass base to prevent damage to the glass edge. The lampwork in all is beautifully done and fills the faceted head of the seal to capacity.

**Russian dahlia paperweight. Dia. 3.9",
Height 2.5".** *Courtesy of The Vienna Art
Auctions, Palais Kinsky, Vienna, Austria.*
$20,000/40,000.

The artistry and content of these lovely weights is
truly remarkable. In this weight the central, pure
white, multilayered dahlia flower is dominant over
the eight other blooms surrounding this central
beauty. The lampworked petals have a central core
of white glass which is then overlaid with a color to
give the petal's edges a lighter hue. The flowers are
set above leaves and stalks which are all encased
within a crown of glass that is not as clear as
lampworked pieces from France of the same
period.

Below:
Side view of Russian dahlia paperweight.
This view shows the slanted facets to the sides with
the body of the weight sitting on an inverted
crystal foot.

Russian paperweight with dahlias and clematis flowers. Dia. 3.5", Height 2.2".
Courtesy of The Austrian Art Auctions, Palais Kinsky, Vienna, Austria.
$10,000/20,000.
All the flowers have a central feature which in paperweights from most other countries would be a millefiori cane to represent the pistils, etc., but in Russian weights the centers are made with tiny pieces of individual glass chippings, creativity and individualism at its best.

Russian paperweight with butterfly and strawberries. Dia. 3.2", Height 1.5".
Courtesy of The Vienna Art Auctions, Palais Kinsky, Vienna, Austria. **$20,000/40,000.**
A bouquet of purple flowers with four strawberries provide a backdrop for the colorful gold and blue winged butterfly. The whole arrangement sits over a white glass ground in this paperweight which has a very low profile caused by a large top facet.

Russian bouquet of 13 flowers in a plaque. Length 5.75", Height 1.5". *Courtesy of The Vienna Art Auctions, Palais Kinsky, Vienna, Austria.* **$40,000/70,000.**

The extraordinary workmanship seen in this plaque is truly amazing. With very little history or expertise in lampwork or paperweight construction, the Russians appear to have produced works of art to rival the very best from the artists making lampworked paperweights at Saint Louis, Pantin, and the Baccarat glassworks in the classic period of the mid-nineteenth century. The caterpillar seen at the bottom of the plaque has been made from a glass material that gives the small creature a very realistic look. The piece has a Cyrillic engraving which translates to (O. F. GROTKOWSKI).

Close up of Caterpillar in Russian Plaque. *Courtesy of The Vienna Art Auctions, Palais Kinsky, Vienna, Austria.*

The body of the caterpillar appears to be made of a material resembling cotton wool, with tiny yellow pieces of glass added individually along and around the body of the very delicate creature. If it were possible to see beneath the caterpillar, I am sure we would find a row of tiny feet.

Russian candlesticks with lampwork. Height 9". *Courtesy of The Vienna Art Auctions, Palais Kinsky, Vienna, Austria.* $6,000/10,000.
Lampworked candlesticks which were made to grace the tables of the rich and privileged in nineteenth century Russia. With the opening up of eastern Europe to free trade, it is possible that other fine pieces will emerge onto the collecting market.

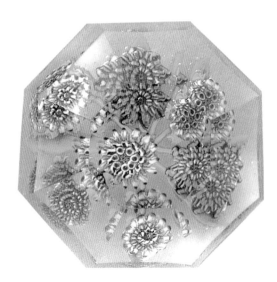

Three Russian paperweights. *Courtesy of The Vienna Art Auctions, Palais Kinsky, Vienna, Austria.* **$2,000/5,000.**
In comparison to the previous lampworked examples from Russia, these three weights would be regarded as more traditional pieces. The flowers are all set in clear glass which has a slight sugary appearance to it with quite a few bubbles of varying size floating around the petals; but, this would not deter most collectors from acquiring a Russian piece for their own collections.

German Paperweights

Information on German paperweight makers is difficult to find, but it has been established that paperweights have been made for many years in the area bordering Germany and Czechoslovakia (Bohemia). The Bohemian weights are reasonably well documented and show a degree of skill and finesse in construction that must have been acquired over many years. Some of these weights are dated, usually showing 1848. However, there appears to be a distinct group of paperweights that lack the quality of the fine Bohemian paperweights in appearance, design, and construction. This suggests that the glassworkers were not as practiced as their Bohemian neighbors. This group of paperweights may well have been made in the latter part of the nineteenth century or early part of the twentieth century and could be an attempt to re-create Bohemian and French paperweights that had peaked in quality and production during the years from 1845 to 1852. The most likely area for these paperweights is Thuringia and in particular a glassworks in the town of Lauscha. A paperweight with close packed millefiori canes with a white plaque and a picture of the local church in Lauscha is held at the glass museum in Wertheim, Germany. The museum has also another weight, without millefiori canes but with a similar white plaque, showing a crude drawing of the Lauscha glassworks, which has been in existence since 1597. The millefiori canes in this paperweight are quite simply made in strong yellow, red, and green colors. There were many other glassworks in this region and almost certainly they made many paperweights with spattered grounds and millefiori canes which could have been sold as souvenirs of the area. In many of these tourist paperweights, there appears a white plaque with the legend *"gruss aus"* and then the name of the area visited. This, when translated from German, reads *A souvenir from.*

Patterned millefiori over spiral cane, c. 1900. Dia. 2.75", Height 1.7". *Courtesy of Gary and Marge McClanahan.* **$350/450.**
Similar in style and cane groupings to the more familiar Bohemian weights from the nineteenth century, but there the similarity ends. This paperweight does not compare in glass clarity or workmanship to the former, but is a creditable attempt to recreate an artifact of bygone years. This paperweight was intended as a gift and not targeted towards the collector market. The glass has many bubbles within the dome, which appears to be a little on the hazy side of clear and the green and orange canes clash in the composition. Overall the weight is a collectible piece and better than average.

Base of patterned millefiori over spiral canes.
The base shows the weight rests on a small area approximately 1" in diameter which is consistent with paperweights from this region of Germany. The bases are usually left in an unpolished state with just the pontil mark removed by grinding. The white spiraling glass is an added attraction on a paperweight, even if it does not reach the standard achieved by the likes of the Saint Louis master glass workers in the mid-nineteenth century.

Macedoine paperweight, c. 1900. Dia. 2.75", Height 1.7".
Courtesy of Gary and Marge McClanahan. **$150/200.**
There are many colorful twists and filigree canes in this weight, set out in a
controlled manner similar to that of the nineteenth century French maker
Baccarat, who produced many paperweights in this classic style. Care and
trouble has gone into the preparation of the canes in this paperweight
before the final dome of glass has been added to seal in the design forever.
At first glance, one could be forgiven for assuming this was indeed a
Baccarat piece, or even a good quality 1930s Chinese weight, but the clues
to the identity of this paperweight are the bright yellow canes much favored
by the German makers, along with the very well made filigree and latticinio
canes in many varied designs and color combinations.

Below:
**Patterned millefiori over yellow ribbon, c. 1900. Dia. 2.8", Height
1.7".** *Courtesy of Gary and Marge McClanahan.* **$250/300.**
It is difficult to place a value on German paperweights as they are so rarely
offered for sale by a dealer or auction house and may sell for much more or
less than the guide I can give. In this weight the canes are spaced over a
bed of yellow ribbon which usually increases the desirability of the piece.
Most German paperweights are thought to be just *European oddities* and
not worth collecting seriously, but the better weights are certainly desirable
and should be allowed space in a mixed collection — if only for the
historical significance attached to the paperweight. The colors are very
powerful with deep royal blue next to dark greens with the old adage *blue
and green should never be seen* ignored in this instance.

Base of patterned millefiori over yellow ribbon.
The idea of ribbon to enhance the motif is very desirable in any weight and
must have been a difficult and time consuming task to achieve. In this
example the glassworker almost achieved perfection but the strength of the
yellow coloring does little to compliment the aesthetics of the piece.

**Double latticinio spiral paperweight, c. 1900. Dia. 2.6",
Height 1.7".** *Courtesy of Gary and Marge McClanahan.*
$150/200.
This is a fine example of latticinio glasswork which has a large blue
and white cane set above a double torsade of white twisted glass
cane that completely fills the weight with the aid of the magnifying
property of the glass dome.

**Spaced paperweight with green flowers, c. 1900. Dia. 2.75",
Height 1.7".** *Courtesy of Gary and Marge McClanahan.* **$150/200.**
Unusual but typical flower type canes that are common in this group of
paperweights from Germany. The canes are set over a deep pink ground of
twisted and filigree canes with open green canes that may have been made
using a crimping tool of some kind. The four lobes of the flowers could
have been made by heating the glass at a lamp and then pressing the soft
glass into a mold or die to get the petal shape and as this design appears
very often in German weights, it is the most likely method of constructing
these repeated flowers. The yellow ribbon covers identical green canes
which are set around a pink and yellow central feature cane that also looks
as though it were made with a molding tool.

**Spaced paperweight with green flowers and blue central cane,
c. 1900. Dia. 2.75", Height 1.7".** *Courtesy of Gary and Marge
McClanahan.* **$125/150.**
A paperweight almost identical to the previous example with just a
couple of cane changes. This indicates that the glassworker had a
certain amount of choice when making the weights and was subject to
the availability of the crimped flowers and canes.

**Spaced paperweight with white flowers, c. 1900. Dia. 2.75",
Height 1.7". *Courtesy of Gary and Marge McClanahan.* $150/200.**
This is another version of the previous weight with the same molded
flowers but this time in white. The flowers are set above a twisted red and
royal blue ground with a central green molded flower cane.

**Patterned millefiori paperweight over latticinio bed, c. 1900.
Dia. 2.8", Height 1.9". *Courtesy of Gary and Marge McClanahan.*
$250/300.**
This paperweight has the strong red, green, and yellow colors associated
with paperweights from Germany. It has a row of canes around the
outside which have seven small elements grouped around a central core
which is reminiscent of classical Bohemian weights from the nineteenth
century. The arrangement of millefiori canes are set above a bed of
latticinio which was a feature in many nineteenth century Bohemian
paperweights and shows the influence of near neighbors Czechoslovakia
on the German paperweights.

Base of spaced paperweight with white flowers.
Through the matte base can be seen what looks like a continuous spiral of
red and blue twisted cane that encircles within the base to fill the void and
produce a background for the white flowers.

**Two row concentric paperweight, c. 1900. Dia. 2.7", Height
1.7". *Courtesy of Gary and Marge Mclanahan.* $175/225.**
Simple and complex canes make up this paperweight from Germany
which may have been made around the turn of the twentieth
century. With the absence of dated millefiori paperweights from this
part of Europe to make comparisons, we must assume that the
volumes were quite small and limited to only a few factories and as
these weights from Germany are quite rare, this would also indicate
that they were made as a very small part of a glasswork's production.

**German two row concentric paperweight, c. 1900. Dia. 2.8",
Height 1.8".** *Courtesy of Gary and Marge McClanahan.* **$250/300.**
An attractive concentric millefiori weight with good color coordination.
Deeply colored royal blue next to white is always a good combination with
the added attraction of pink and yellow canes with white strands of filigree,
in a type of cane that is commonly found in German weights of this period,
c. 1900.

**Six flower in spiral white glass, c. 1900. Dia. 2.7", Height
1.8".** *Courtesy of Gary and Marge McClanahan.* **$125/150.**
This popular set up of six molded flower canes arranged around a
white pastry mold cane has sunk into the blue and white spiral bed,
perhaps deliberately, but the whole piece looks untidy and was
probably a mistake.

Side view of spaced millefiori over yellow petals.
German paperweights usually show a low profile with very little variation in
diameter and height dimensions.

**Spaced millefiori canes over yellow flower petals, c. 1900. Dia.
2.8", Height 1.8".** *Courtesy of Gary and Marge McClanahan.*
$125/150.
The green canes with filigree of a lighter color are set over a three
dimensional yellow flower with a white center. An attractive and innovative
fantasy flower displaying a high degree of skill on the part of an anonymous glassworker.

Scottish Paperweights

The Scottish glass industry, and art glass in particular, received inspiration from a Spanish immigrant family by the name of Ysart. They helped to create a glass paperweight industry that has firmly established Scotland as the world leaders in the production of quality paperweights with millefiori and lampwork. Until the arrival of the Ysarts, Scotland did not have any historical connection with millefiori paperweights. The family arrived in Scotland in 1915 to seek out the many opportunities for skilled glassworkers that existed at that time. Salvador Ysart, 1875-1955, the head of the family, had learned his craft whilst working at several French glasshouses and the Leith Flint Glass Company and another Scottish glassworks prior to joining the Scottish firm of John Moncrieff Ltd. in 1922. Salvador's artistry was encouraged by the management at Moncrieffs, who allowed him a free hand to experiment with decorative glassware. This glassware was eventually marketed under the name Monart Ware. The name Monart is derived from a combination of letters from the family name Ysart and Moncrieff. As they came of age, Salvador's sons all joined the firm as his assistants. The brothers Paul (1904-91), Augustine (1906-56), Vincent (1909-1971), and Antoine (1911-1942) all became skilled glassworkers under their father's guidance. It was the eldest brother Paul who started to experiment with paperweights containing millefiori canes and later lampwork. Although chastised by his father for wasting his time with these objects, Paul continued in his spare time and developed a style and expertise that would soon be followed and copied by many others in this field of glass artistry. By the late 1930s, Paul's work was so good it was often confused with classic antique French paperweights. He began signing his weights with a PY cane to identify his work.

Over the years, the family working group began to go their separate ways. Antoine was killed in a traffic accident in 1942 and in 1946 Salvador left Moncrieffs with Vincent and Augustine to start a company called Vasart, derived from a combination of the first letter in each of their names and the last three in Ysart. Paul stayed with Moncrieffs but was allowed much greater freedom to follow his chosen passion for paperweights and in 1955 the American dealer and collector Paul Jokelson contacted Moncrieffs to become the sole importer of Paul's work into the USA. This gave the company and Paul a welcome boost and exposure to a fast growing body of collectors in America. His weights were becoming recognized and sought after worldwide. In 1963, Paul left Moncrieffs to take up the position of training officer at the Caithness Glassworks.

Under the guidance of Paul, many of Scotland's finest paperweight makers learned their trade. Among his students were Peter Holmes (who went on to help found Selkirk Glass), John Deacons, William Manson, and many more, all to become successful artists in the world of paperweights.

Today, the volume producers in Scotland are Perthshire Paperweights, Selkirk Glass, and Caithness Glass. Although these major glasshouses turn out thousands of paperweights every year, they still produce weights in limited and special editions that are eagerly collected by enthusiasts throughout the world. Early and limited editions from these large producers command high prices when appearing at auction and have proved to be a sound investment for collectors, plus the advantage of being beautiful objects to display and admire.

Paul Ysart concentric paperweight. Dia. 3.1", Height 2". *Author's collection. $750/1,000.*

Paul Ysart never dated his paperweights, so trying to put a date on them is difficult. Ysart himself admitted that because he had made so many over a very long career, he could not identify precisely when he had made a particular piece. Fluorescence testing is a great help and is 95% accurate in differentiating paperweights made during his working career at Moncrieffs, Harland, and Caithness. The early paperweights made during the Moncrieff period were made with a glass that is not crystal clear. The glass appears to have a dark tinge that does not detract from the beauty or value of the weight but can be seen clearly when placed next to a heavy lead crystal weight. This weight was an early piece made at Moncrieffs, but could have been made anytime between 1930 and the early 1960s. The canes are simple cogs and rods that are bundled together to make a more complex cane but placed precisely, a trait that was to become synonymous with Paul Ysart paperweights. Even at this earliest stage in his career, he proved to be quite meticulous with his cane set ups and it is very rare to find an Ysart with slipped or distorted canes.

Paul Ysart paperweight. Dia. 3.2", Height 2.3". *Author's collection.* **$750/1,000.**

A good example of the precise set ups found in Ysart weights. The lengths of latticinio and ribbon canes are all precisely cut to an equal length, the canes are the same size, and then neatly set into the mold before being picked up with a hot gather of glass to seal the design in. The accuracy with which Ysart collected his set ups from the mold even surpasses the antique French and English makers of the classic period; it is almost unheard of to see a Paul Ysart weight which is even slightly off center.

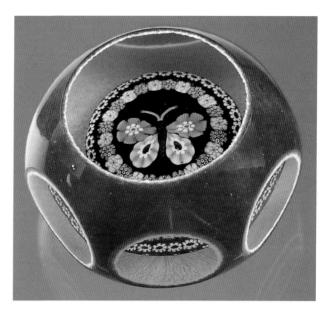

Paul Ysart double overlay butterfly paperweight. *Courtesy of Colin Mahoney.* **$3,500+.**

This is the famous overlay paperweight made in the 1930s that was photographed and included in the first edition of *Old Glass Paperweights* by Mrs. Evangeline Bergstrom. The weight was thought to have been French because of the fine quality of construction. The weight is signed PY which Mrs. Bergstrom mistook for the signature of a French glassworker. The overlay is made by marvering the hot weight in powdered glass chippings. This would be repeated several times until the desired depth of color was achieved, the weight was heated at the glory hole to fuse the glass chippings over the paperweight to create an overlay of firstly white glass and then the outer red layer. The problem inherent with this very simple method of overlaying weights is that it leaves ragged edges on the faceted windows after grinding. Although this paperweight is very rare and highly desirable, the method was not pursued at the time and only two other overlays have been recorded to the author's knowledge.

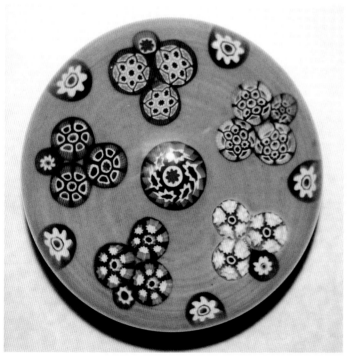

Paul Ysart color ground paperweight. Dia. 3.2", Height 2.2". *Courtesy of Terry and Hilary Johnson.* **$750/1,000.**

This weight was part of the Parkington collection and displays the original Monart Glass label that helps to date the weight to the Moncrieff period. Paul Ysart made paperweights on various colored grounds. The colored ground is a very desirable and attractive feature in an otherwise simple design.

Top view of Paul Ysart overlay paperweight.

This is a truly superb example of Paul's early work during his Moncrieff Period. The butterfly is without fault, as are the two rows of precisely set canes which are sized to perfection. The ragged edges to the overlay can clearly be seen on the top facet of this wonderful piece. The PY signature cane sits in the inner row of canes.

Salvador Ysart mushroom paperweight with torsade. Dia. 3.5", Height 2.25". *Courtesy of Norah and Alastair Petrie.* **$750+.**
This paperweight is almost certainly a unique piece from Salvador Ysart. The weight could have been produced at anytime during his career, but as a high degree of skill and technique is required to produce a mushroom shape and a torsade, it is possible it was made after he left the Moncrieff Glassworks to found his own company in 1946 and before he died in 1955. The green and white torsade adds a touch of antiquity to this very rare weight which was probably made as a frigger. Paperweights were not made by Salvador in any great quantity whilst at Moncrieffs, but after founding the Vasart company he became involved in weights and inkwells commercially. The main Scottish Museums in Perth and Edinburgh have been shown this weight and both agree, it is by Salvador, but they have never seen a similar piece before.

Salvador Ysart Doorstop. Dia. 6", Height 5", Weight 6.5 pounds. *Courtesy of Norah and Alastair Petrie.* **$750+.**
This is a partially hollow doorstop that was made at the Moncrieff Glassworks between 1925 to 1929. It can be reasonably accurately dated to this period as the weight has a label on the base that says *Monart Ware, Doorstop,* the name was changed after 1929 to *Monart Glass.* The owner of this remarkable piece has researched it thoroughly and suggests that it is a one off piece made for a Monart collector as he has found no mention of doorstops being made in any of the Monart reference books.

Salvador Ysart butterfly paperweight. *Courtesy of a private collector.* **$750/1,000.**

In the field of lampwork and paperweight making, Salvador never quite reached the heights achieved by his son Paul, but examples of his work are keenly sought by collectors everywhere because of their rarity. This butterfly weight is one of only a dozen or so known to collectors. This one has wings made from flattened millefiori canes and a green aventurine body. The butterfly sits over a spattered ground within a garland of canes.

Robbie Burns sulphide with pink and white feathered canes by Paul or Salvador Ysart. *Courtesy of Colin Mahoney.* **$1,200+.**

A very rare sulphide with a spectacular feathered garland of millefiori canes which was created by pulling a steel pick through the hot canes. The canes have so far not been matched to any signed Paul Ysart weights but do match the previous Salvador butterfly paperweight precisely.

Salvador Ysart butterfly paperweight. Dia. 3.2", Height 2.5". *Author's collection.* **$1,000/1,200.**

This butterfly is quite well made, but not as meticulously put together as Paul's butterflies. The weight is unsigned, which is normal for Salvador, but paperweights with this arrangement of rods, laid flat over the orange ground, is somewhat perplexing. A paperweight with the same millefiori rods has been found in another weight that is thought to have been made by Paul Ysart. Paul did experiment with sulphides and it is probable that father and son shared canes during their working relationship at Moncrieffs.

Rare Ysart feathered two row concentric paperweight. *Courtesy of Colin Mahoney.* **$1,000+.**

The same feathering appears in this weight which has the same fluorescence as the previous paperweight and appears to have been made by the same hand during the Ysarts career at the Moncrieff Glassworks in the 1930s. Both weights fluoresce the same as signed Paul Ysart paperweights made in the 1930s. My personal view is that the feathered paperweights were made by Paul as it would seem that it was he who was experimenting with design and sulphides in paperweights, whereas Salvador's butterfly, with its pink and white canes, tends to look a little heavy handed in comparison to these two beauties.

Vasart two tier flower paperweight. Dia. 3.5", Height 2.25".
Courtesy of a private collector. **$400/450.**

A rare lampworked flower, possibly by Salvador Ysart, made during the
Vasart period but only tentatively attributed to him as the Vasart company
had begun to make many production weights, therefore it could have been
made by any one of the skilled glassworkers at the factory. This is true of
the attribution of most paperweights originating from the bigger glass
producers. Unless they are signed by the artist, you have personally
watched it being made, or have evidence to that effect, the weight is best
described by the name of the factory rather than a particular artist. It is easy
to convince yourself that you recognize a particular artist's style. Still, when
labeling your collection, name the factory rather than the artist.

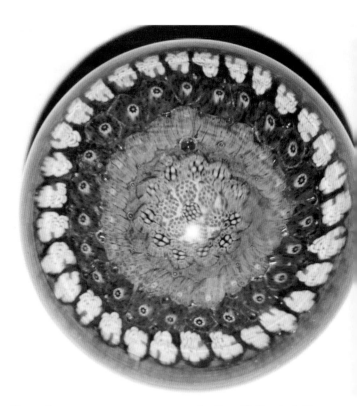

Vasart four row concentric paperweight. Dia. 3", Height 2.3"
Courtesy of a private collector. **$350/450.**

This is a very rare and good example from the Vasart factory as the outer
row of white canes are an attempt to create a white rose. The slices of canes
are stacked against each other in the style of the antique Bohemian
paperweights and the result is a good attempt to recapture the techniques
involved in rose canes. Unfortunately, the coloring of the whole weight, with
the garish orange canes, does little to enhance the beauty of the weight.

Close up of Vasart four row concentric paperweight with rose canes.

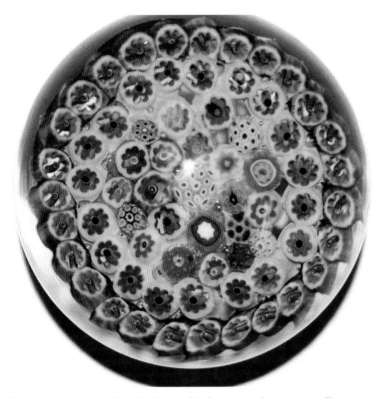

Vasart paperweight. Dia. 3", Height 2". *Courtesy of a private collector.*
$400/500.
A well made weight from Vasart with a good selection of canes in the close pack central part. Two rows of canes circle the central area of this quite hard to find Vasart paperweight.

Vasart inkwell. Dia. 3.8", Height 4". *Author's collection.*
$650/800.
This is not a good example of a Vasart inkwell. Such inkwells are normally attributed to Salvador Ysart. The cane arrangement leaves a lot to be desired and it is possible this piece was made by another production worker learning the trade. The pieces made by Salvador are of a much higher quality and command prices in excess of $1000 at auction.

Paul Ysart and Salvador inkwell. *Author's collection.* **Paul's inkwell, $2,000+; Salvador's inkwell, $1,000 +.**
Two very good examples of a father and son's artistic interpretation of the ever popular decorative inkwell. That on the left is by Paul and shows a close packed assortment of canes with a garland of simple hollow cogs with an orange center. A very simple cane but used to great effect when set as precisely as these in the matching top and base in this lovely example. The inkwells that are normally attributed to Salvador show very little variation in size and style. They are always constructed almost identically to this piece, with a variation in colors only. They can be found in orange, blue, green, pale blue, an almost brown color, very pale yellow, and other slight variations of these colors. The neck of the bottle has radiating color that is a feature of the stopper as well. Paul identified this style and shape as the work of his father.

Paul Ysart inkwell. Dia. 4", Height 4.25". *Private collection.* $1,500/2,000.
Paul Ysart made inkwells in two very distinct shapes. This shape is very similar to his father's inkwell and it is possible he could have made this style while working alongside his father at the Moncrieff Glassworks. Father and son must have been an influence on each other to a certain degree, having worked together for so many years of their careers.

Paul Ysart paperweight. Dia. 2.9", Height 1.9". *Author's collection.* $750/1,000.
The cane colors are not usually compatible, but in this weight with a blue ground and close packed center the colors do not detract from the weight's aesthetics.

Paul Ysart inkwell. Dia. 4", Height 4.3". *Private collection.* $1,500/2,500.
The difference in quality between Salvador/Vasart and Paul's inkwells is obvious to everyone who collects paperweights. The precise nature of the settings and canes makes this a very desirable piece. This inkwell also has a red flashing to the stopper and neck which is also the sign of a superb craftsman, knowledgeable of his materials and tools.

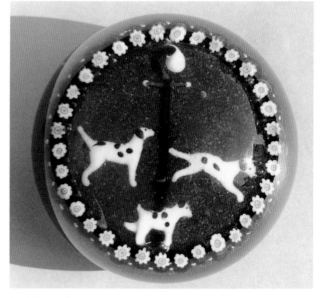

Paul Ysart dog paperweight. Dia. 3.5", Height 2.3". *Courtesy of Terry and Hilary Johnson.* $1,500/2,000.
This is a very rare paperweight and is probably unique. The dogs are superbly made in two dimensions. One has its leg up a lamppost, doing what dogs do. Paul was known to have made several whimsical pieces and this piece has been identified by people who worked with Paul during his long career making paperweights.

Paul Ysart butterfly paperweight. Dia. 3", Height 2". *Courtesy of a private collector.* **$1,200/1,500.**
A fantasy creature, like all Paul's butterflies, he never tried to imitate nature with a realistic copy of the natural butterfly. This garlanded weight, consisting of white millefiori canes and a green aventurine body on the butterfly, is a lovely example of these rare paperweights.

Paul Ysart red flower paperweight. Dia. 3", Height 2.2". *Courtesy of a private collector.* **$750/1,000.**
Stunningly framed against a royal blue background, the red flower centers the paperweight beautifully. The canes in the outer row are a mixture of cogs and tubes spaced evenly around the flower.

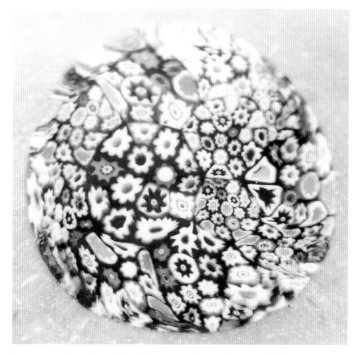

Paul Ysart miniature paperweight with complex central cane. Dia. 2", Height 1.5". *Author's collection.* **$500/750.**
A fine example of an Ysart miniature with a central cane that Paul described as his *stones*. These were samples he kept for reference, but occasionally he would use one in a weight.

Close up of Paul Ysart miniature with complex central cane.
The close up of the *stone* reveals that this very complex cane is comprised of approximately 12 canes which are also complex. They are bundled together to make a cane with around 150 individual elements.

Paul Ysart spaced paperweight. Dia. 3", Height 2". *Author's collection.* **$650/800.**

This paperweight is signed with a H cane to signify it was made during 1970/75 when Paul worked in his own glassworks at Harland farm near Wick, Scotland. Although the company existed for only six years, the production was quite prodigious. With the assistance of Willie Manson, this small company could make up to 200 weights per week. Most of the weights with a PY signature were destined for the USA, but those with an H cane were sold in the UK. Even though Paul was past retirement age, his love of his work and his vast experience meant that he produced some of his best paperweights at this time. The "H" cane also refers to the trading name Paul used for a short time, which was Highland Paperweights.

Scottish Butterfly paperweights. *Author's collection.*

A variety of butterflies The two on the left are made by Paul Ysart and the two on the right are by John Deacons. The top right was made by John during his J glass days. The smaller piece in the center is signed PY, but is a fake signature cane with a dropped Y and a variation in the color of the P&Y signature cane.

Close up of Paul Ysart butterfly paperweight.

Complex, mixed colored canes are used to create the wings of this pretty butterfly. The canes are gently flattened to shape the wings and dark green aventurine is used for the body.

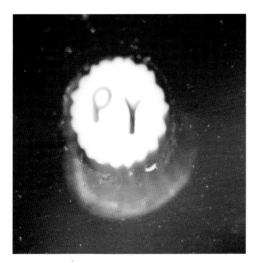

Fake Paul Ysart signature cane.
This cane is a 20 cog cane which Paul Ysart did not use for his signature canes and is known to be a fake cane, made by someone other than Paul Ysart. The easy way to recognize a fake Ysart weight is to look closely at the colors of the P and Y. The P is a yellow/brown and the Y is a red . This color difference is found in all Paul Ysart fakes, regardless of whether the Y is dropped or the weight has a ground flat base, or if the pontil is left unground, and regardless of however many teeth there are to the cane. The difference in the letter colors is the only constant in all types of fakes. The *easy way* was first published in the *Cambridge Paperweight Circle Newsletter* in December 2000 by a very knowledgeable collector of Ysart paperweights, Terry Johnson.

William Manson junior double snake paperweight. *Courtesy of the Manson family.* **$1,000/1,200.**
Two very realistic green scaled snakes rest on a sand and pebble ground. The snakes are made using green aventurine with bands of scales encircling the body of the snake. Two very nice flowers with striped leaves gives this piece extra appeal.

Willie Manson double lizards paperweight. *Courtesy of the Manson Family.* **$750.**
Willie was a good and very talented student under Paul Ysart and, after learning his craft at Harland and later with Caithness Glass, he and his family now have their own studios making paperweights with millefiori and lampwork inclusions. The two lizards are made using a red /brown aventurine color which is very effective over this mottled green ground. The inclusion of the blue and yellow flower adds a nice finishing touch to this special piece.

Manson Inkwell. *Courtesy of Manson family.* **$1,100.**
This inkwell is a collaborative piece by the two Williams and incorporates a fine spray of yellow daisy flowers with leaves and backed by a blue flash overlay to the base. This very fine piece is multi faceted with a matching stopper. William Manson Junior has learned well the exceptional skills taught by his father and this family team can only go on to greater challenges.

Allan Scott, born 1958, Lampworker. *Photo courtesy of Caithness Glass, Inveralmond, Perth, Scotland.*

Allan Scott's career in paperweight making began in 1975, with Perthshire Paperweights. First applying for a weightmaking position, he found that they had all been taken, but he was offered a job as a trainee lampworker (because he had qualifications in art from school) by Anton Moravec, the manager at that time. He trained under the supervision of Angus Hutchinson.

The head glassmaker at the time was John Deacons, who asked Angus to make some flowers with special 3D petals. John had worked out how to make the specialist petals by studying photographs of antique French weights. Angus refused for various reasons, but Allan offered to make them with Johns guidance in his spare time. The working relationship with John Deacons flourished until John decided to leave to form his own company, J Glass. A few months after getting the company started, John asked Allan to leave Perthshire and work with him as a lampworker. With orders flooding in for their lampwork creations, John took on two more workers: George Constable to help John and Archie Anderson to do the cutting and faceting. Other workers who had also left Perthshire to help at the J Glass studios were Harry McKay and Brian Lawson. In 1983, J Glass was put into receivership and closed.

Allan Scott applied to Caithness Glass for a position as a lampworker but, as no department for lampworking existed at that time, he was offered a job as storeman. After nine months, Colin Terris and the company directors decided that Caithness should expand into lampworked paperweights and the obvious choice to head the lampwork section was Allan Scott, who very shortly had three trainees working with him, including Rosette Flemming, who still works at Caithness today. Today Allan spends most of his time making exhibition pieces for Caithness, usually with Harry McKay, born 1954, who also joined him at Caithness Glass.

A 1997 Caithness red flashed mixed lampwork paperweight by Allan Scott & Harry McKay. *Photo courtesy of Caithness Glass, Inveralmond, Perth, Scotland.*

This is a beautiful example of the superb quality lampworked paperweights that are currently being produced by the world's largest quality paperweight producer. Allan Scotts artistry at the lamp helps to keep this volume glassmaker at the forefront of technical innovation. The red flashed base highlights the spray of delicate flowers in blue, white, and yellow. The flowers have a lightness to the petals and stamens which only a person with many years of training and experience at the lamp can ever hope to achieve. Harry McKay is the hot glass man who puts the design within the hot glass and it is his skillful dexterity with the pontil rod that creates the final shape of the paperweight.

Caithness pink rhododendron flowers by Allan Scott & Harry McKay. *Photo courtesy of Caithness Glass, Inveralmond, Perth, Scotland.*

A wonderful paperweight with flowers and petals that have a 3D effect. The petals are created with a clear crystal inlay to give the effect of three dimensions. This technique was taught Allan by John Deacons. The petals curl around the invisible crystal inlay to great effect.

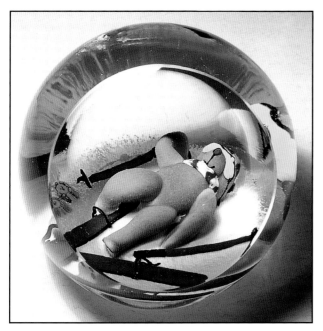

A 1998 Caithness skiing teddy bear by Allan Scott & Harry McKay. *Photo courtesy of Caithness Glass, Inveralmond, Perth, Scotland.*
A skiing teddy bear takes a tumble on the slopes. Adorned with a scarf of red and white and yellow goggles, the bear lies on a scattered snow ground.

A 1998 Dahlia torchwork paperweight by Allan Scott & Harry McKay. *Photo courtesy of Caithness Glass, Inveralmond, Perth, Scotland.*
Many of the paperweights Allan Scott and Harry McKay are involved with are usually at the cutting edge of innovation and style. In this piece, the lampworked flowers have been melted on the outside of the crystal ball, just enough to leave the detail of the flowers with soft edges and trailing leaves. This weight combines visual beauty with being able to feel the design.

Jack Allen spaced paperweight. Dia. 2.8", Height 2.1". *Author's collection.* **$200/300.**
Jack Allen was apprenticed to the Ysart brothers at the Vasart glassworks in 1948 and stayed with the company until 1974. During this time, the company changed hands and names from Vasart to Strathearn and then to Perthshire Paperweights. This paperweight was made around 1970 and can be considered quite rare. His signature cane, JA, is in the central orange cane. Jack Allen was the first person at Perthshire to be allowed to place his own signature cane alongside the Perthshire P. This paperweight was probably made during the Strathearn or Vasart period and features clusters of canes over a gold aventurine ground.

John Deacons, 2000, double overlay blue flower paperweight. Dia. 3.25, Height 2.25". *Courtesy of a private collection.* **$350/500.**
John Deacons continues to produce these beautiful double overlays with single, double flowers and bouquets at prices that are within the reach of all collectors. The petals of this flower show the three dimensional look he has achieved by wrapping the petal around a crystal rod at the torch. The weight is fancy cut exposing the thick layer of white glass. The flower sits above a crown arrangement of latticinio canes. All John's weights are now signed and dated.

137

John Deacons, 2000, double overlay rose paperweight. Dia. 3.24", Height 2.25". *Courtesy of a private collection.* **$350/500.**
Made in the style of a *thousand petal rose*, the rose is well made with unfolding, red petals. Overlaid in a similar color shade of red, over a thin layer of white glass, gives the inside walls of the weight a rosy hue.

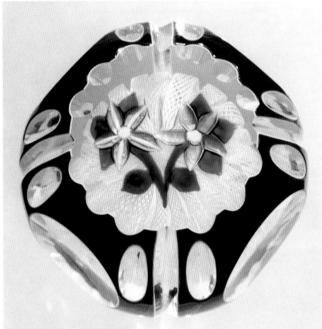

John Deacons, 2000, double overlay double flower paperweight. Dia. 3.25", Height 2.25". *Courtesy of a private collection.* **$350/500.**
There are simple flowers in this weight, but with the very distinctive purple overlay and deep vertical cutting through the color, this weight has great appeal to the collector. Being set over a crown of latticinio rods to cushion the motif also adds appeal to these stylish paperweights.

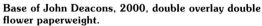

Base of John Deacons, 2000, double overlay double flower paperweight.
The skill involved to make a weight of this quality is clear to see. John Deacons has a long history of working at his art, for himself and for Perthshire Paperweights. All the skills learned over many years show in the meticulous way this paperweight has been constructed. In all of Deacons's work, he has always considered the base of a weight to be as important as the dome. In this paperweight, the base is as attractive as the top.

John Deacons inkwell/perfume bottle. Dia. 2.5", Height 3". *Author's collection.* **$75/100.**
All Scottish paperweight artists and glassworks have at some stage of their careers made this type of inkwell/ perfume bottle. With the passing of the ink pen, the inkwell is now solely decorative, but could still be used for perfume. The thistle cane in the top is only one of the signature canes used by John Deacons and is similar to the thistle used by Willie Manson during his Scotia days. John Deacons's thistle has a solid shaped green cane to form the body of the thistle, whereas the Manson thistle body is made from a millefiori cane.

Perthshire Paperweights, 1980, inkwell. Dia. 3.5",
Height 5". *Author's collection.* **$450/600.**
The base and stopper are matching close packed arrangements in this very fine example of an inkwell. Beautifully set on a dark blue ground and then encased in Perthshire's crystal clear glass.

Perthshire Paperweights perfume bottle. Dia. 2.75",
Height 3.5". *Author's collection.* **$75.**
This perfume bottle has the Perthshire P in the center of the concentric rows and was made in the 1980s. Precisely constructed and made as an unlimited production piece. Elegant blue threads are encased the length of the stopper.

Perthshire Paperweights quadruple overlay, 2000. *Courtesy of Perthshire Paperweights, Crieff, Scotland.*

This is a stunning design of pink blossoms on woody stems over a blue ground. The four overlays are colored white, red, white, and blue which are then cut and faceted to reveal the individual colors beneath each layer of glass. This is the first and only one of this type to be made this year. This is the type of weight which can show real investment potential in the space of just a few years. A beautiful work of art from Perthshire Paperweights.

Perthshire Paperweights signed millefiori and twists paperweight. Dia. 2.8". *Courtesy of L.H. Selman Ltd., Santa Cruz, USA.* **$155.**

A precisely made patterned millefiori with twists of cane to separate the panels of millefiori segments. All millefiori canes are set in steel templates before being handed over to the glassworker for encasing. This ensures there is no movement of the design during encasement. The weight is signed with a letter P in the central cane and has side and a top facet.

Perthshire doorknob. Dia. 2.4". *Courtesy of L.H. Selman Ltd. Santa Cruz, USA.* **$175.**

Radiating twists surround the three concentric rings of canes with two further rows around the edge of the Knob. The whole piece is set within a brass mounting. An elegant piece to grace the home of any paperweight collector.

Perthshire Paperweights snowdrop paperweight. Dia. 2.5", Height 1.75". *Author's collection.* **$250/350.**

A single snowdrop and bud over six leaves is encased in clear glass in this near perfect representation of the woodland flower. The central millefiori cane has a letter P in the center and the cane is attached to five white petals with striping to the petals, just like the natural flower.

This is a limited edition of 150 pieces made by Peter Holmes. Selkirk Glass produce many abstract paperweights as well as millefiori and lampworked pieces. The piece is engraved with edition number and date on the base.

Selkirk Glass marbrie paperweight. Dia. 2.5", Height 1.7". *Author's collection.* $350/450.
This Marbrie style of paperweight was first made by St. Louis, c. 1850, in France and the French version has become an extremely rare and expensive weight. This Selkirk Marbrie was an exercise to see if the style could be repeated. The Selkirk piece is also becoming a hard to locate paperweight for those collectors who want an example of every style in their collection. The weight itself is as good as the antique version. To create the striping effect, a steel pick is pulled through trailed glass lying on the surface of the hot body of glass.

Selkirk Glass inkwell by Peter Holmes. Dia. 3.25", Height 5.25". *Author's collection.* $350/500.
This abstract design has a base of glass chippings with a matching stopper. The inkwell is signed in the stopper with a PH cane.

Selkirk Glass surface butterfly paperweight. Dia. 2.8", Height 1.9". *Author's collection.* $200/250.
The solid body of the weight is decorated on the outside of the weight with a butterfly and flowers that are flush to the surface with a light covering of glass to smooth and seal the surface. The paperweight is signed with a PH cane to say it was made by the joint owner of Selkirk Glass, Peter Holmes. Peter Holmes learned his craft at Caithness Glass while Paul Ysart was the training officer in charge of the new paperweight makers. They became great friends and Paul instructed Peter in many of his secret methods used in paperweight making. The simple flowers adorning this very different piece are copies of the simply made flowers Paul made for use in his bouquet weights.

141

Chinese Paperweights

The history of paperweight making in China begins around 1930 and although China has a glass industry that goes far back into history, paperweights were completely alien to the Chinese before c. 1930. Paperweights made from this time were for export only. The province of Shantung (Shandong), in the north of China, is the region where most paperweight production takes place. The lampwork in the 1930s was probably done at home by outworkers who were used to producing small flowers at the lamp for decorative uses in the local glasshouses. This is also suggested by slight variations in the construction of the petals and leaves of these early pieces; but, now paperweights and glass with millefiori decoration have turned into a substantial industry in this region with The Zibo Zhaohai Light Industrial Products Company Limited the main producer of paperweights and decorative glassware.

The Chinese have developed a reputation for copying almost any item at a much reduced cost due to the very cheap labor force. These skills were utilized by American importers who sent out several antique French and American weights for the Chinese to attempt to copy. The weights that were to be copied included American poinsettias, Baccarat pansies, primroses in various colors, and garlanded posy weights. Nearly all the copied antique weights were made on a clear or latticinio ground, either in white or occasionally one can be found over a bed of yellow strands. The majority were usually uncut but several faceted weights are known. These 1930s copies of antiques were not signed. However, in later years the United States insisted the country of origin must be shown on all imported goods and so the weights began to be scratch signed, and eventually labeled *Made in China* or sometimes were shown with three small white tablets inserted reading *Made in China*. A certain degree of success was achieved with weights containing millefiori canes and lampworked flowers, but the overall appearance could not match the original antiques when placed alongside for comparison. The main failing was the clarity of the glass due to the numerous bubbles and amount of detritus within the dome of the weight. The glass composition of Chinese, French, and American weights is very different. French and American weights have a high lead content which adds to the clarity of the glass whereas the much lighter soda glass favored by the Chinese usually has a slight yellowish tinge in the early weights. Nineteenth century European makers had managed to clean the glass almost entirely of any impurities. The Chinese, however, due to costs and technical factors, could not match the standards set by the European and American antiques.

Almost all the lampworked copies of flower weights were sent to the USA with only an odd few finding their way across the Atlantic to Europe. These antique copies are now considered to be very collectible with finer pieces selling for around $400. The weights that were shipped to Europe tended to be of the millefiori type which have never reached the same prices as the antique flower copies. Most millefiori pieces, even if well constructed, rarely sell for more than $60, with most selling around $25.

Since the 1970s, Europe and America have experienced an explosion of imported cheap paperweights from China. A box of 12 weights could be bought at wholesale for around $18. The glass in these weights is far superior to the earlier pieces, having almost optical clarity and with well-made flowers, bugs, birds, and snakes enclosed within. In 1975, several of these weights from around 1970 found their way into respectable auction houses and held their own amongst other modern paperweights and were sold for $60 each. I wonder if these 1970s better quality weights have appreciated in value over the last twenty-five years, as I have been unable to establish if any have been offered at auction recently.

Paperweights are still being exported to most countries and sold through gift shops and antique fairs, where the prices are often inflated by unknowledgeable dealers to extreme heights and usually remain unsold. Today's trade price for these imports is still very low at around $5 each; but, they can very often be spotted on antique stalls priced from $30 to $80.

Red poinsettias. *Author's collection.*

This is an example of the type of paperweight that was sent to China for copying. The weight on the left is obviously the copy, with the piece on the right being the antique from the Boston and Sandwich Glass Company. At the beginning of the copying era, the weights sent to America were of a very poor quality with bubbles and detritus in the glass dome. The Chinese have a history of glass making, but the composition of the glass in paperweights made in the 1930 to 1940 period is extremely poor, which may be due to the use of too much alkali in the mix. The best way to describe the glass is "sickly." The poinsettia copy would retail for around $50, but the genuine article would sell for $500 or more.

Red poinsettia, c. 1930. Dia. 2.75", Height 1.75". *Courtesy of Gary and Marge McClanahan.* **$100/150.**
This must be a very early example, judging by the "sickly" glass. The dome can be seen full of many small bubbles, almost clouding the glass. The flower is well made with all the petals in the right places but the glass lets the weight down badly. It is interesting that there are many collectors of these weights, including many large dealers in the US and UK, possibly for their historic values more than their monetary value. The yellow millefiori cane centering the weight is a cane that can be found throughout the history of Chinese weights and still turns up in weights made yesterday.

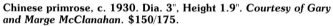

Chinese primrose, c. 1930. Dia. 3", Height 1.9". *Courtesy of Gary and Marge McClanahan.* **$150/175.**
It is very difficult to put a value to these early Chinese paperweights as so few actually come up for auction. Early weights seen at antique and dealer fairs show a huge difference in pricing by the individual dealers. I have personally paid as little as $20 each, but I would gladly pay $300 or more for a quality piece. As you will see in the following examples, the Chinese were not afraid to produce the same primrose style in a multitude of colorways, with or without buds and a variation in petals.

Faceted red poinsettia, c. 1930. Dia. 2.75", Height 2". *Courtesy of Gary and Marge McClanahan.* **$200/300.**
Almost identical to the previous red poinsettia but this piece has six side and a top facet. Still with the same "sickly" glass and yellow millefiori center.

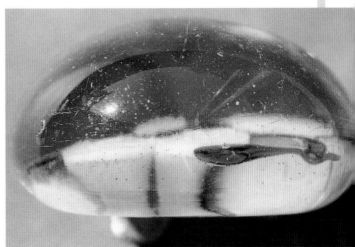

Chinese primrose, c. 1930. Dia. 2.75", Height 1.75". *Courtesy of Gary and Marge McClanahan.* **$150/175.**
The double layer of petals in slightly different colors could have made for a very pretty and expensive weight, but the glass has many nicks and scratches due to the low esteem in which these gift weights are held. I have no idea of the prices the original importers tried to achieve with these copies in the 1930s, but because of the poor quality of the glass they must have been retailed at the lower end of the market — as are the Chinese weights that are still being imported today.

Side view of Chinese primrose.
The side view shows the low glass dome of the weight with a slight yellow tinge to the glass. This slight discoloration of the glass is typical of the early Chinese copies and this imperfection was not removed until the 1950s.

Chinese primrose paperweight, c. 1930. Dia. 2.75", Height 1.7". *Author's collection.* **$150/175.**
The Chinese made many variations of each flower, with and without a bud, and in many different colorways. This weight has the almost standard yellow central cane which is still used in weights made today. The central cane can have a slightly different make up, which when combined with slight differences in the petal construction, may indicate that the lampwork was done by different people. It is thought that outworkers made the lampwork which was collected by an agent who then sold the work to the glasshouse.

Chinese primrose paperweight, c. 1930. Dia. 2.75", Height 1.75". *Courtesy of Gary and Marge McClanahan.* **$200/250.**
Another primrose weight with a bud and a different central cane. The colors in this weight are deeper and with an added bud the weight would cost a little more to buy.

Chinese primrose paperweight, c. 1930. Dia. 2.75", Height 1.75".
Courtesy of Gary and Marge McClanahan. $175/225.
A primrose with red and yellow petals and a bud. The bud balances the weight nicely and is always a welcome addition on flower weights.

Chinese primrose over latticinio, c. 1930. Dia. 2.75", Height 1.7".
Author's collection. $225/275.
This weight has been set over a bed of yellow latticinio strands which adds interest and desirability to the otherwise ordinary paperweight. The strands of yellow glass in these early examples are very loosely woven, but in later versions the techniques were mastered to a very high degree of skill. The main petals have a hint of pink showing through to give a delicate appearance to the lampwork.

Chinese pink primrose paperweight, c. 1930. Dia. 2.75", Height 1.7". *Author's collection. $175/225.*
This weight has very pretty white petals with a hint of pink blush showing through. The glass and composition of the weights started to get better as production and skills increased towards the end of the importation of these copies, which was probably around the end of the 1930s.

Chinese primrose paperweight, c. 1930. Dia. 2.75", Height 1.7".
Courtesy of Gary and Marge McClanahan. $175/200.
The petals on this lampworked flower clearly show a much more rounded petal against similar examples of the same type of primrose. This would indicate that more than one person was making the lampwork with the finished article being encased at the main glassworks.

Chinese red and white primrose over latticinio, c. 1930. Dia. 2.75", Height 2". *Courtesy of Gary and Marge McClanahan.* **$150/175.**

This is a very loosely made latticinio example that must have been an early attempt at this technique. The flower itself is not of the quality that was eventually achieved by the Chinese glassworker.

Chinese paperweight, c. 1930. Dia. 3", Height 2". *Courtesy of Gary and Marge McClanahan.* **$450/500.**

Eventually the Chinese did make good copies of the French and American antique weights they had been asked to copy. This is a very well made paperweight, even by today's high standards. This weight and several more of the following weights are the most highly desirable of all the Chinese paperweights from the 1930s and have become very rare and collectible. This lampworked and faceted piece has been replicated to an almost mirror image of the New England Glass Company original. It would take an expert on American paperweights to distinguish between the two, except that the Chinese version of this paperweight still has the tell tale sugary glass with a hint of yellow. The weight is precisely faceted to a good standard with the flower sitting over a well constructed latticinio bed.

Side view of red and white primrose over latticinio.

The side view shows the very loosely made latticinio and lampworked flower. The sides of this weight have a distinctive narrowing towards the base, which is quite typical of Chinese paperweights from the 1930s to the present day but variations to the norm can be found with low domes and wide flat bases. The matte finish to remove the pontil mark can be found on 99% of Chinese weights, old and new.

Chinese paperweight, c. 1930. Dia. 3", Height 2". *Courtesy of Gary and Marge McClanahan.* **$450/500.**

A nosegay of four red and yellow flowers with leaves made in the New England style with a garland of pretty red and green millefiori complex canes, spaced precisely around the edge of the weight. Another row of red and white canes, which are interspersed with blue and white complex canes, adds interest to this delightful copy of an antique American paperweight.

Chinese pansy paperweight, c. 1930. Dia. 3", Height 2". *Courtesy of Gary and Marge McClanahan.* **$350/450.**
This Chinese copy of an antique Baccarat pansy from c. 1850 is almost as good as the original. The lampwork is beautifully precise with just a couple of leaf tips that are untidily finished, but the petals of the flower are extremely well made The whole lampwork set up is centered perfectly but alas the glass lets the finished weight down with many bubbles visible all over the weight. The latticinio is also of the highest standard.

Chinese faceted pansy paperweight, c. 1930. Dia. 3", Height 2". *Courtesy of Gary and Marge McClanahan.* **$450/500.**
This is another example of the best the Chinese glassworkers had to offer and it looks as though they have almost achieved a perfect product. Most of the bubbles have been eliminated and the lampwork and setting is more than adequate; but, the weight also displays the almost classic tell-tale sign that this is a Chinese copy: the glass covering dome shows that slight yellow tinge that the classic French weights never had. However, this piece is a welcome addition to anyone's collection due to its historical position in the paperweight world.

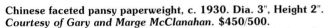

Chinese primrose over latticinio, c. 1930. Dia. 3", Height 2". *Courtesy of Gary and Marge McClanahan.* **$500/600.**
This is a superb example from an unknown Chinese glassworker who has created a collectible paperweight that could stand comparison with most modern paperweights. Although this piece was a mass produced item, it must have been created at the very end of the production run to have achieved such a high standard of competence. The whole weight has been precisely constructed with beautifully crafted petals of a pale lilac hue with the top layer a slightly darker lilac. The central yellow cane is the now familiar cane made from small yellow tubes, surrounding a red center. This primrose flower has a small red and yellow bud and five dark green petals all set over a precisely made yellow latticinio ground. Paperweights made in China from this early period of around 1930/40 do not get any better than this.

Chinese butterfly paperweight, c. 1930. Dia. 3", Height 2".
Courtesy of Gary and Marge McClanahan. **$250/300.**
This Chinese butterfly weight is the first the author has ever seen and
it is almost impossible to put a realistic valuation to this very rare
paperweight. Rare it may be, but the weight shows all the faults the
Chinese had with their glassmaking, which suggests that the piece
was an early 1930 example of a Baccarat butterfly copy. The green
bodied butterfly is hovering over a bright yellow primrose with
several green leaves beneath the petals. The wings of the butterfly are
made by pinching a rod of glass and dotting it with colored glass
chippings to add some color to the wings. The antenna have been
added in slightly the wrong place with one slipping beneath the head.

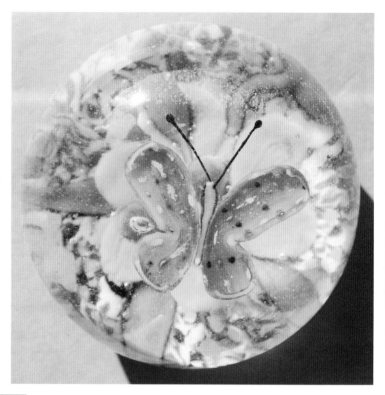

**Chinese patterned millefiori paperweight, c. 1930. Dia. 2.75",
Height 1.4".** *Courtesy of Gary and Marge McClanahan.* **$50/60.**
Paperweights made in the early 1930s all display this yellow cast, as can be
seen on this weight. Although it is well made, with a good selection of
millefiori canes, the pale colors of the canes let the weight down. Unlike the
paperweights made in Europe and the USA in the nineteenth century,
nearly all Chinese weights lack the depth of color achieved by the
glasshouses the Chinese were trying to imitate. As a general guide to dating
these weights, it is reasonable to assume that anything with this yellow
caste was made before the Second World War. The clearer glass weights
were imported into Europe and the USA during the 1960/70 period when
the glass became much clearer, but the quality of the product declined.

**Chinese carpet ground paperweight, c. 1930. Dia. 2.75", Height
1.5".** *Courtesy of Gary and Marge McClanahan.* **$30/40.**
The low domes of these early paperweights from China also help to date
the weights to before World War II, as does the bubbly glass mix in this
weight. The canes have the six arms common in many weights and can be
found in a multitude of colorways. The millefiori concentrics and other
weights made from millefiori canes are more reasonably priced due to the
vast numbers made. This type of paperweight from China can still be found
in considerable numbers worldwide and, with very few exceptions, they are
not considered to be collectible.

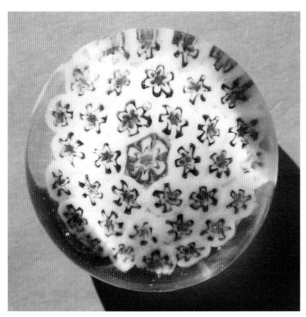

Chinese white carpet ground. Dia. 2.5", Height 1.3".
Courtesy of Gary and Marge McClanahan. $30/40.
Another variation of the carpet ground paperweight with three
rows of the same white, red, and blue canes.

**Signed Chinese close packed paperweight. Dia. 2.5", Height
1.5".** *Courtesy of the Portia Gallery, Chicago. $80/100.*
After the Second World War ended in 1945, the United States
enforced a trade embargo on all communist countries and it was
after this embargo was lifted in 1958 that all imported goods were
obliged to be labeled with the country of origin. Originally, many
Chinese weights could be found with just a scratched *Made in China*
on the base of the weight, but eventually the familiar white glass
blocks were introduced and used for a number of years. The modern
imports from China now have a stick on paper label to denote
country of origin. From the early 1980s, the Chinese paperweight
quality deteriorated due to the enormous volumes churned out and
did not recover until consumer demand necessitated a better quality
product in the late 1980s. This weight has an attractive array of
miscellaneous canes with the added attraction of a signature cane.
This weight is worthy of addition to a collection just for the signed
tablets enclosed within the paperweight. The weight is unlikely to
appreciate much in value, but as an historical weight it is worth
keeping.

Chinese close packed paperweight. Dia. 2.7", Height 1.5".
Courtesy of Gary and Marge McClanahan. $50/60.
This is a very good example of a close pack with a multitude of clear and
well made canes. The composition and clarity of the glass suggests that it is
a later weight made after 1980. The same types of canes used before the
war continue to be used right up to the present day. This is a weight that
should be collected as an example of the improving Chinese artistry.

**Chinese painted butterfly paperweight, c. 1930. Dia. 2.75",
Height 1.7".** *Author's collection.* **$75/100.**

The next few paperweights are not made with the traditional materials we
associate with glass paperweights such as millefiori or lampwork, but they
do conform to the shape and size of the more familiar collector's weights.
Surprisingly, they are much sought after by dealers and collector's alike.
The weights are made from a light soda glass and probably originate from
the same sources as the 1930s millefiori and lampworked copies. The off-
white ground has a painted scene of flowers and a hovering butterfly. This
paint must be compatible with the molten glass, as I have never seen a
weight of this type with an annealing problem but the paint does show
signs of crizzling on many of this type of weight. The material used was
perhaps a finely ground colored glass paste which was then applied with a
traditional painting stick or brush. The finished tablet was then encased
with a dome of glass to enhance the scene.

Base of Chinese painted butterfly paperweight.

The base has been ground to remove the pontil mark and as usual has
been left unpolished with a matte finish which is still the way modern
Chinese weights are made. The weight shows no signs where the two
halves were brought together to make a whole weight.

Chinese painted bird paperweight, c. 1930. Dia. 2.7", Height 1.7.
Author's collection. **$75/100.**

Almost any outdoor scene can be found on these Chinese weights and this
one has a swallow- tailed bird flying over a plot of blue, red, and yellow
flowers with greenery and brown stalks. A close examination reveals that
the painted strokes have stretched and expanded slightly during the
encasing process, but does not detract from this miniature work of art.

**Magnum Chinese painted heron paperweight, c. 1930. Dia. 3.8",
Height 2.7".** *Author's collection.* **$150/250.**

A good realistic likeness of a red headed heron standing in front of a tree
with branches, leaves, and red blossoms. Although these paperweights
were once quite common around the flea and antique markets, realizing
only a few dollars each, they have become increasingly hard to find. As
this piece is of a rare magnum size, the price is considerably enhanced.
Fortunately, many of these painted weights have survived without to
much bruising and damage and it should still be possible to build a varied
and unusual collection of this type of paperweight before they are
gathered up into private collections forever.

Chinese painted cigarette ashtray, c. 1930. Dia. 3.5". *Author's collection.* $75/100.
A parakeet sits at the bottom of this ashtray, once an everyday household object.

Chinese painted bus paperweight, c. 1930. Dia. 2.7", Height 1.7". *Authors collection.* $100/120.
Most of the painted weights from China are of a floral nature, but occasionally something different does turn up such as this scene with a bus and mountains. The style of the bus, with its opening roof vents, dates the weight to the 1930s. The red paint of the sun shows signs of crizzling through expansion during the reheating process and is quite commonly found on many of these painted weights.

Chinese painted butterfly paperweight, c. 1930. Dia. 2.7", Height 1.7". *Courtesy of Gary and Marge McClanahan.* $50/60.
A large butterfly hovers over crudely painted flowers in a paperweight that looks as if the painter had been interrupted and never completely finished the scene before it was sent away for encasing.

Chinese river scene paperweight, c. 1930. Dia. 2.7", Height 1.7". *Author's collection.* $80/100.
A simply painted river scene with brown buildings in the foreground and a peasant poling his canoe down the river.

Chinese painted schooner paperweight, c. 1930. Dia. 2", Height 1.5". *Courtesy of Gary and Marge McClanahan.* **$60/70.**
This schooner weight is probably the most common of the Chinese painted weights and is slightly smaller than the floral weights. It is quite crudely painted which suggests that more than one artist was at work on this type of weight.

Chinese fish tank toy. Approximate size 1.25". *Courtesy of the Portia Gallery, Chicago.* **$20/30.**
It was thought for many years that these small objects were paperweights, but current opinion is that they were intended to be placed inside ornamental fish tanks. Once under water the cube becomes transparent with the fish appearing to swim without restraint. The material used would appear to be a chalk or powdered glass substance that is compatible with glass as the two elements have fused together perfectly without any sign of stress or annealing fractures. The green weed is made from pulled glass and the main body of the glass has a distinctive yellow tinge. As this glass object appears to conform to a paperweight shape, they have been acquired by paperweight collectors as curious Chinese oddities.

Chinese hunter painted paperweight, c. 1930. Dia. 2.7", Height 1.7". *Courtesy of Gary and Marge McClanahan.* **$100/120.**
A proud hunter stands to have his portrait painted and the Chinese characters to the right of the paperweight may tell us when and where this was made. However, having asked several Chinese friends to decipher the words, all they could tell me was that the man was a *"hunter of tigers in the mountains."*

Chinese fish tank toy or paperweight. Dia. 1.75", Height 1.5". *Courtesy of Gary and Marge McClanahan.* **$50/75.**
This paperweight contradicts the fish tank theory as it has been faceted all over with a large top window for viewing the interior design and was obviously made as a decorative paperweight. However, it is made in the same style and with the same materials as the fish tank toys. The petals of the pink and yellow flowers have been painted with a heat resistant paint or paste.

Chinese Buddha faceted paperweight. Dia. 1.75", Height 2.25". *Courtesy of Gary and Marge McClanahan.* **$75/100.**
This Buddha sits on a green ground cushion which rests on a bed of yellow filigree. The weight is faceted all over with diamond cutting, so it must be a paperweight.

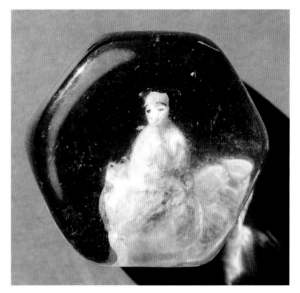

Chinese fish tank toy. Approximate size 1.25" dia. *Courtesy of Gary and Marge McClanahan.* **$30/40.**
The majority of these small objects that author has seen are cube shaped, which would seem to have been the easiest shape the glassworker could make and, as they were destined for the bottom of a fish tank, the shape did not matter. Any that are faceted or shaped other than cubes must have been made to be displayed around the house.

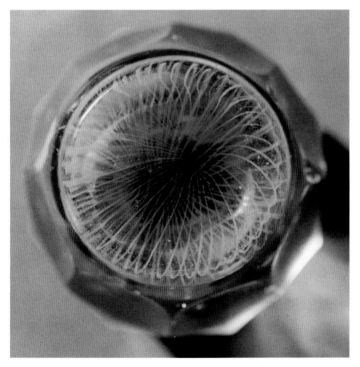

Base of Chinese Buddha paperweight.
The base has very fine strands of yellow filigree and in this case the base has been polished to allow the filigree to be seen. Most Chinese paperweights do not have the bases polished, with this weight being one of the exceptions.

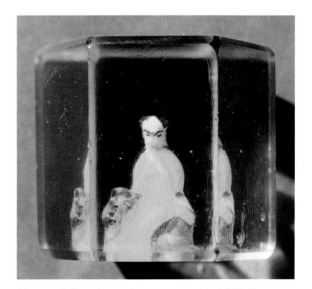

Chinese fish tank toy. Approximate size 1.25" dia. *Courtesy of Gary and Marge McClanahan.* **$30/40.**
A Chinese man sits in a chair dressed in a bright yellow gown. This bright bilious yellow can usually be found in most Chinese paperweights as the color has not changed from the 1930s weights to present day production.

153

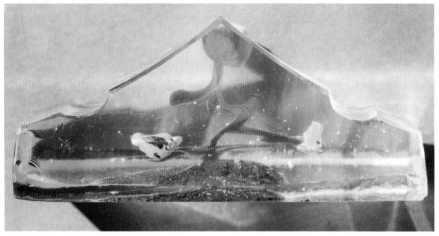

Chinese chopsticks rest. Length 2.5". *Courtesy of Gary and Marge McClanahan*. $30/40.
Two small yellow birds sit on a red branch over a green ground in this useful object.

Right:
Chinese 1970s millefiori paperweight. Dia. 2", Height 2.75". *Author's collection*. $10.
In the early 1970s many of the Chinese weights lacked any kind of quality. The weights were just bundled rods of garishly colored millefiori canes. This indifference to quality production, even in cheap gift weights, led to a decline in sales and it was not until the late 1980s that the quality began to improve, with the glass dome becoming very clear and with lampworked items becoming extensive in variety and the skills used.

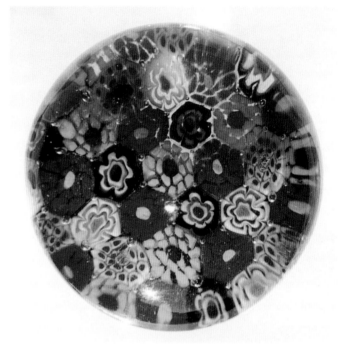

Millefiori chopsticks rest. Dia. 2.3". *Courtesy of Gary and Marge McClanahan*. $30/40.
This chopsticks rest has canes, in a style that has changed very little from the 1930s to the present day, which makes the dating of this object difficult. The glass is quite clear, so it could have been made yesterday or 30 years ago.

Right:
Chinese red flower over latticinio paperweight, c. 1970. Dia. 2.7", Height 1.7". *Courtesy of Gary and Marge McClanahan*. $60/80.
This 1970s paperweight has been well constructed, but the flower petals and bright yellow latticinio strands clash.

154

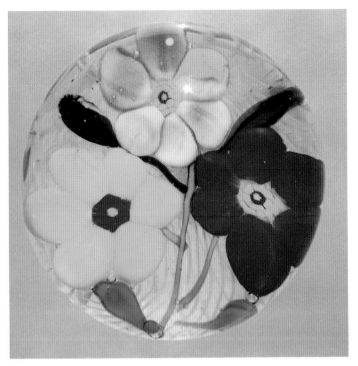

Chinese three flower paperweight, c. 1970. Dia. 2.5", Height 1.5".
Author's collection. **$30/40.**
Three flowers and a bud on a loose bed of latticinio in this style of Chinese weight which has been produced by the thousands every year since the 1970s. The quality of this loosely constructed paperweight is still poor.

Chinese stylized flower with two hovering bees, c. 1980. Dia. 3.2", Height 2.5". *Author's collection.* **$30/40.**
During the 1980s, this very common paperweight could be bought from the local giftware wholesaler for $30 a dozen. The main reason for the Chinese ability to produce weights at such economic prices was the development of a tool known as a crimp. This device forms the petals of a flower without lampworking individual parts. The tool can be as simple as a block of wood with pieces of metal or nails protruding or a sophisticated tool with shaped tines for petals. This device can then be pressed gently into soft colored glass over a bed of clear glass, the metal spikes will leave an outline of a colored petal when withdrawn. This tool shapes a multitude of petals quickly. These crimped paperweights came in a variety of styles and colors. Some would have birds, frogs, or small fish inside and proved a very popular gift in the tourist areas and seaside resorts the world over and at a price that was affordable by everyone. The glass is a heavy lead crystal and has lost the yellow tinge associated with Chinese weights from earlier years.

Chinese red flower paperweight. Dia. 2.75", Height 3".
Courtesy of Mr. and Mrs. T. Stokes. **$20/30.**
From the late 1980s, the Chinese glass industry made gift paperweights that had improved in artistry and glass clarity. Many of the stylized flowers show great dexterity and have formed a base for paperweights that have improved yearly.

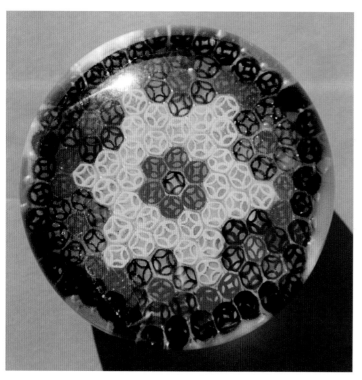

Magnum Chinese paperweight. Dia. 3.5", Height 2.25". *Courtesy of Gary and Marge McClanahan.* **$100/150.**
This is a very large millefiori paperweight with a very precise and complex set up. The canes are of a very simple construction with the same cane being used in a variety of colors, including the bilious yellow and the outer circle of canes in a rarely used black color.

Chinese footed bird paperweight. Dia. 2.75", Height 3.25". *Courtesy of Gary and Marge McClanahan.* **$80/100.**
Three white doves sit amongst foliage in this weight. The lampworked doves are neatly made with red eyes and beaks attached in the right places.

Chinese footed anemone flower. Dia. 2.75", Height 3.25". *Author's collection.* **$60/80.**
At the end of the 1980s and early 90s, the quality of workmanship and glass clarity was such that it was amazing that paperweights could be produced for such a low base price of around $5 each; but, with the help of the crimping tool the Chinese could produce and send paperweights throughout the world by the ship load.

Chinese anemone flower. Dia. 2.9", Height 2.25". *Author's collection.* **$30/40.**
This is probably the most common of all Chinese imports and can vary in size from a miniature to a magnum. They can be found almost everywhere, from flea markets to good quality antique fairs and emporiums. The colors can be white, yellow, red, blues, or pink.
As with most of the flower weights with numerous petals the flower has been made with a crimping tool.

Chinese pink amaryllis flower paperweight. Dia. 2.9", Height 2".
Author's collection. $50 plus.
Of all the modern Chinese weights I have seen this amaryllis paperweight displays workmanship of the highest quality. The stamens and flower heads are finely crafted and a similar paperweight is illustrated in Patricia McCawley's book *Glass Paperweights* which was first published in 1975 by Charles Letts of London. McCawley says that *"a very fine imitation of a white Amaryllis with yellow stamens, was sold by auction for $70. If they are well made and attractive, they can hold their own amongst other modern paperweights in a collection"*. This pink version of the same paperweight that McCawley describes is of equal quality and deserves recognition as such. It would be interesting to see how much one of these Amaryllis paperweights would realize in an auction today.

Chinese Amaryllis paperweight. ***Author's collection.***
This version of an Amaryllis flower has slightly deeper pink hues to the very fine petals.

Chinese fish paperweight. Dia. 2.75", Height 2.6". *Author's collection. $10.*
This attractive gift paperweight can be bought at my local charity gift shop for $10 and is representative of a mass produced paperweight made for just a few dollars but with enough appeal to be made by the Chinese glass industry in the tens of thousands.

Chinese 1999 lizard paperweight. Dia. 3", Height 2.3". *Author's collection.* **$10.**

It is quite amazing to think that this paperweight has been made in China, sold to an importer in England, and then sold at retail for just $10. This weight is sold through my local charity shop, but they have been turning up on antique fairs and even on eBay the internet auction site, where they have fetched in excess of $60 plus.

1999 Chinese reproduction of a nineteenth century Baccarat butterfly and garland (test piece). *Private collection.*

A garland of green and white simple canes around the well made butterfly, constructed in the Baccarat style of the nineteenth century, makes this a desirable paperweight even though it has been made as a copy. The row of millefiori canes have been pulled down under the weight to the center which tidies the pontil area.

1999 Chinese reproduction of a nineteenth century Baccarat bouquet paperweight (test piece). *Private collection.*

This is a superb attempt to recreate an antique Baccarat masterpiece. The lampwork has been faithfully reproduced with a thousand petal rose as the main attraction with a yellow wheatflower, a pansy, and blue primrose with two other buds to compliment the scene. The flowers are set above green petals and two stalks. As with most copies it is not as good as an original, with several faults such as the blue primrose floating adrift with no stalk to anchor it to the bouquet and with several large bubbles. However, with the original Baccarat antiques selling for around $20,000, this copy may be the only way many paperweight collectors can get to own a similar piece.

1999 Chinese reproduction of a nineteenth century Baccarat clematis flower and garland (test piece). *Private collection.*

In this weight the garland has been poorly set. The canes, which are typical red and white Chinese canes in use today, have moved during the encasing process. The weight has not been made as carefully as the previous two weights and the appearance of the paperweight is not as well constructed as in the previous examples.

1999 Chinese made in the style of Yaffa Sikorsky-Todd and Jeffrey M. Todd (test piece). *Private collection.*

This very attractive paperweight has been reproduced in the style of American artists Yaffa Sikorsky and Jeffrey M. Todd. White millefiori canes with red centers decorate the tree as blossoms. The tree is growing over a green spattered ground with the addition of colored flecks to the rear as distant flowers.

Left:
Page from Chinese trade catalog. *Courtesy of Kevin Holt.*

This page is from a Chinese trade catalogue that lists over five hundred different paperweights made with millefiori and lampwork motifs. Some are very good examples of weights made from around the world in many different countries, from the last one hundred and fifty years. Remember, do not be fooled by a pretty face.

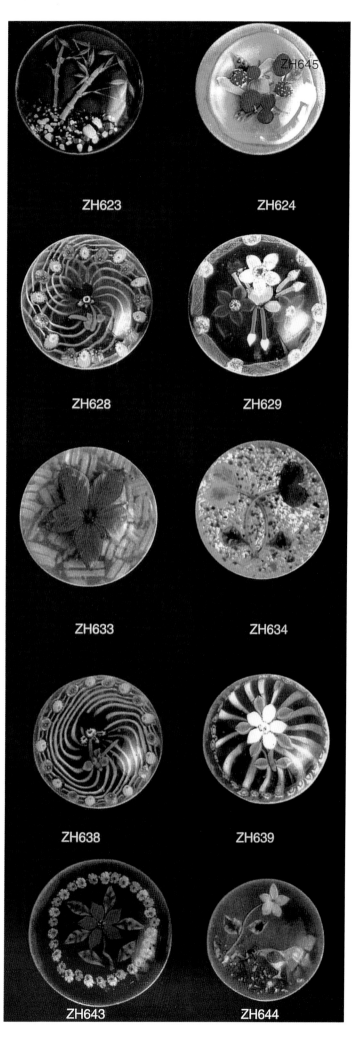

ZH623 ZH624

ZH628 ZH629

ZH633 ZH634

ZH638 ZH639

ZH643 ZH644

ZH645

Recommended Reading

Bedford, John. *Paperweights*. New York: Walker and Company, 1968.

Hall, Robert G. *Old English Paperweights*. Atglen, Pennsylvania: Schiffer Publishing, 1998.

_____. *Scottish Paperweights*. Atglen, Pennsylvania: Schiffer Publishing, 1999.

Hollister, Paul, Jr. *Encyclopaedia of Paperweights*. Santa Cruz, California: Paperweight Press, 1969.

Jargsdorf, Sybille. *Paperweights*. Atglen, Pennsylvania: Schiffer Publishing, 1991.

Kulles, George. *Identifying Antique Paperweights*. Santa Cruz, California: Paperweight Press, 1985.

_____. *Identifying Antique Paperweights (Lampwork)*. Santa Cruz, California: Paperweight Press, 1987.

Mannoni, Edith. *Classic French Paperweights*. Santa Cruz, California: Paperweight Press, 1984.

McCawley, Patricia K. *Glass Paperweights*. London: Letts and Co., Ltd., 1975.

Melvin, Jean S. *American Glass Paperweights and Their Makers*. New York: Thomas Nelson, Inc., 1967.

Russian Glass of the 17th-20th Centuries. Corning, New York: Corning Museum of Glass., 1990.

Sarpellon, Giovanni. *Miniature Masterpieces Mosaic Glass 1838-1924*. Munich, Germany: Prestel, 1995.

Von Brackell, Peter. *Paperweights: Historicism, Art Nouveau, Art Deco, 1842 to Present*. Atglen, Pennsylvania: Schiffer Publishing, 1999.